52 Weeks of Creative Living

Inspiration for Your Creative Soul

––––––––

Malcolm Dewey

52 Weeks of Creative Living – Inspiration for Your Creative Soul
Copyright © 2017 by (Linspire 124 CC t/a Malcolm Dewey Fine Art)

Printed in by Linspire 124 CC
(www.malcolmdeweyfineart.com)

Discover More:

Also written by Malcolm Dewey:

An Artist's Survival Guide
The Art of Content Marketing
How to Loosen Up Your Painting
An Artist's Guide to Plein Air Painting

Painting Courses:
Learn to Paint With Impact
How to Loosen Up Your Painting
How to Solve Painting Problems
Form Acrylics to Oil Painting in 5 Easy Steps
Plus Start a Free Painting Course with Malcolm

Podcast:
An Artist's Journey Podcast

Dedication

To Kerrin and the boys. Also to my parents.

Contents

Introduction

There are times in an artist's life when a well-chosen word can make a big difference. Fact is, artists face a precarious existence. I do not mean financially, although that could be the case too. I do refer to the emotional state of the artist.

By the way, when I refer to 'artist', I include all creative people. The trials faced are similar for all of us, so the emotional state governs everything. How artists see the day ahead, from the moment they wake up in the morning, can make or break the day.

I am no different. By some accounts (like my wife's) I can be moody, negative, positive and cheerful. In no particular order. All before breakfast. Perhaps you can relate?

An attitude-adjusting event is very important when the day looks perilous. Sometimes a good cup of coffee can do the trick; other times a little more is required.

I have found that a few pages of reading can help too. I especially like a short, sharp read at the beginning of the day. I am a big fan of those books that have a pithy piece of advice or story to illustrate a lesson. All wrapped up in a short chapter.

Even better if it is a big book with plenty of chapters like this. I can then get my quick fix when required. Light bulb! Why not write the book I want to read. And so the idea for this book came about.

Now, I cannot guarantee an epiphany in every chapter. They are rare things indeed. Hopefully I can help you with a new perspective when required. A smile here or there. A shared experience. A crisis survived.

I recommend having this book in the little room for a private moment. Or wherever you can steal ten minutes to get your read.

I do hope that you enjoy this book and have a wonderful creative year ahead.

Thank you,
   Malcolm

Chapter 1:
But I'm Not Ready!

Looking back on past New Year's Days, there are distinct life stages that I have pulled through. The twenties when I was dirt poor, in debt and happy. New Year's Day would often be welcomed with a slight stagger from overindulgence the night before. A day spent resting and enjoying the moment.

In the thirties New Year's Day became a frustrating wait for the working year to begin. I had joined the rat-race. I had started a family and it was time to make a future for all of us. This meant working for money basically. Run, run, run. Not a happy decade overall and it passed so quickly. I have to work it out in my mind and picture the good moments with my family. But deep down, there is the icy feeling that I had too many worries clouding my days.

Then the forties. Slowly I realized that a change was required. The connection between art and my spirit had to be restored. I was not an office worker by nature. This lifestyle is fine if it brings you joy, but for me the daily grind and worries of professional work had locked me away. My sense of humor and spirit had been whittled down. I was tired.

Resolution: paint regularly and redevelop my painting style. The goal was to exhibit paintings by the end of the year. With this resolution established I began to follow it through. It was perhaps the first time I had really taken action on my New Year's resolutions.

To cut a long story short, by the end of 2009 I had exhibited paintings at a Christmas fair. Sales were better than expected. I had made the step required and began to see potential.

Well, that is all history now. I am working full-time painting and teaching art. Writing books too evidently. It all seems so bizarre. But wonderful too. I know it is not a big deal in the scheme of things, but to me it was a massive risk. I never expected to turn what is a hobby for most people into a living.

I will go into this process more in this book, but for now these lessons stand out:

1. It is never too late - within reason of course. But, if physically and mentally you are able to do what you want to do, then put that process into action.
2. Focus on the ONE thing you need to do right now. I had one resolution. More than that and I get distracted.
3. Kick the time-wasting habits step by step. For me, the first action step was to cut down on watching TV. Eventually I got rid of cable altogether. No internet TV either. This gave me extra days in the month. It is huge!
4. Be patient and make steady progress. Success is a process, not a destination. Stopping because it

is taking too long is to guarantee failure. Persisting is to guarantee success - one day at a time.

5. Read more non-fiction books. Unless you have a full time mentor, you will need to learn from somewhere. New lessons come from many sources, but books are my number one resource.

Happy New Year!
Now go get 'em tiger!

Chapter 2:

Find Your Sweet Spot

The summer break over December could not have come at a better time. I expect most people have similar feelings when the year's travails have built up together with the expectations of a well-earned rest. In my case, this amounted to two weeks away from my studio and office. No internet either. Other than Christmas preparations, I had undivided time for painting. I had decided that this time would comprise of plein air painting only.

I have a suitcase converted into a portable plein air studio. It can carry my tripod, pochade box, roll of brushes, paints and bottles of brush cleaner plus the few other bits and pieces that make painting easier. With this kit I can set up my plein air expedition almost anywhere.

Why just plein air? First off, I had some bad habits to clear up from the past year. So many other commitments to a painting life leads to adaptions to my painting process. This can lead to excessive details and other sort of fiddles that distract me from getting to the essence of a painting.

Overworking a painting is perhaps one of the biggest frustrations an artist can face. How to say what is necessary and no more. This plagues writers, poets, movie makers and probably any creative pursuit one can take up. Plein air painting is a way of getting back to the essentials. The foundation.

The summer heat means having a routine for early starts to the day. At six AM I was at the beach setting up my pochade box. While other early beach goers were taking their walks and swims, I was looking out for compositions to paint. In summer, this golden light created wonderful *contre jour* opportunities.

Since I was facing east, I had the sun reflecting off the sea directly in front of me. People were walking along the water's edge or venturing into the sea. By standing in an elevated position, either on a dune or even the car park, I could look down towards the sea. This meant I still had brilliant colours coming from the sea and sand - greens, blues, golden sand, and foaming waves of yellows and violets.

The challenge to identify these colours, mix them from a limited palette of primaries, and put them on the panel is the highlight of the plein air experience.

The process is one of intuitive painting. Rapid paint application - but never done recklessly. You have to concentrate to see what is actually going on in front of you. The temptation is to simply paint waves as you might know them from pictures.

This approach does not teach us anything. Plein air teaches us to really see, interpret paint's true colours, and capture the truth of the scene. This is a learning experience filled with excitement that no art book or video can match.

Once you take on the plein air painting approach, you will see, for example, that fanciful seascapes of translucent waves curling over in greensih-yellow hues are simply concoctions far removed from reality. Pretty pictures yes, but in truth they are as surreal as any Dali painting.

If truth in representational painting is what you seek, then plein air impressions and studies are essential. You can even paint the ugly and everyday scenes around you and show them to be worthy subjects. This is where the art comes in and transforms the scene into its essence of hues, shapes and values.

Between six and seven AM, I could complete two panels then break off until the late afternoon. This daily routine was a wonderful way to spend my time free of distractions. Of course, another benefit of plein air is that my studio works will benefit too.

Plein air works are references in themselves. The outdoor painting experience also adds to my artist's memory. Sensations experienced first-hand are accessible in the studio too, which translates into larger paintings that have that sense of immediacy and truth.

With a renewed sense of purpose, I look forward to another year of painting, learning and sharing my art experiences with you.

Chapter 3:
What Art Demands from You
(or Every Dog Gets Its Day)

What does an artist expect from life? To make a living, get rich or simply make art and do a day job? It is a personal choice. What about the artist who struggles valiantly, but never seems to break out of obscurity?

For this artist, each sale is a lifeline and the waters are treacherous indeed. It seems likely that bitterness and regret may dog this artist's path forever. In this case, there is perhaps no better example than the musician Rodriguez.

Sixto Rodriguez - the mysterious musician from Detroit, was a Seventies singing icon in South Africa and a symbol of counter-culture for our white youth for at least three decades. He performed timeless folk songs that are as poetic and powerful today as they were in the seventies.

Rodriguez's story made headlines in 2013 with the Oscar- winning documentary feature, *Searching for Sugarman*. If you have not seen the movie, then please do so. No matter what your taste in music, the human story is so compelling and moving that it will leave a lasting impression.

Here is a highly talented artist. His music in the early seventies is as good as Bob Dylan's, but nobody takes notice. Rodriguez lives in humble circumstances working as a labourer. His dream to become a recognised musician falls flat in the USA.

Perhaps the truth is that Rodriguez never dreamed of fame and fortune at all. However, in Australia and especially South Africa, his music became massively popular in the seventies and continued unabated.

An urban legend, carried on from word to mouth, was that Rodriguez was dead. Suicide... That is until he was discovered by a couple of South African fans in the late 90's! Rodriguez is still alive and living in Detroit. Humble home. No car. Basic wage. Despite royalty checks being sent to his record label, Rodriguez has not received any money or recognition for his music. He was also unaware of his fame in South Africa.

This changed when Rodriguez was persuaded to come to South Africa and perform in a series of concerts in 1998. All the concerts were sold out. Yet, in spite this success, Rodriguez was happy to go back to his humble home. Despite netting six-figure earnings from the concerts, he gave most of it away to friends and those needier than him.

If he was bemused by his success back then he should have been stunned by the worldwide fame to come when *Searching for Sugarman* won the Oscar for best documentary in 2013. Suddenly Rodriguez was in demand everywhere - even in the USA.

Yet Rodriguez did not use the money for personal wealth. He still gave it away. He stays in the same house. He still has no car and still lives with the basics. To this artist, it is all about performing his art. As Rodriguez says about fame and fortune - **all you need is food, clothing and shelter. Everything else is icing**.

For those artists chasing wealth, Rodriguez may seem crazy. Perhaps some are appalled at his lifestyle. But why? Rodriguez seems to appreciate that people do not own things. Things own people. By attaching ourselves to outcomes and material goals, we are always going to be uneasy with life.

Attachment leads to fear and suffering. Loss of freedom. The only thing Rodriguez has in his life is his ability to create art. He loves to share this art with the world, not for reward, but because it is his calling.

Let the rewards come and go. Change is the only constant.

The next time you feel like complaining, or get frustrated or bemoan your situation, think of Rodriguez. Be humble and grateful for life and the opportunity to make art. Love what you do and give freely. That is all that is required of us.

Chapter 4:

What My Surrealist Cat Taught Me about Acceptance

It is that time of summer when the humidity and tempers have risen to dangerous levels. The sort of weather that makes people say and do crazy things, then regret them later when the consequences come back to haunt them.

I once read that the widespread use of air conditioning significantly lowered the divorce rate in Texas. Presumably this applies to anywhere that suffers from very hot summers. Makes sense really. The heat also affects productivity at work. Even something like painting for a few hours becomes frustrating when you have to stand under a cold shower to keep sane.

My studio does not have air conditioning. Winter is not a problem with a basic heater sorting the chill out. But high humidity cannot be escaped. It saps creativity and the patience to press on when things are not working out. What to do when the heat wave starts to run for days on end?

Well there is the wisdom that work should be done early and then late in the day. The unpleasant middle part of the day being sacrificed to a siesta. Empires may not have been built on this idea, but it seems like good sense to me.

A few hours of repose during the heat of the day, phone off the hook and away from traffic, can only help to keep a person sane. Another plus is that energy can be replenished for a late afternoon flurry at the easel.

It is also best to avoid all potentially annoying situations. Driving, waiting, phone calls and paying bills all conspire to kill creativity. Avoid them all until you have cooled down or, preferably, until autumn arrives.

Our family cat has demonstrated its talent for dealing with the heat. Consider that a cat is covered in fur and should suffer in the heat. Compared to our dog that pants away like a machine while simultaneously drooling like a fool, the cat takes it all very calmly.

Just yesterday, I observed our cat stretched out on my wingback chair. Its hind legs were touching the floor, its back draped over the seat while one of its front paws was extended to the top of the chair, its claws embedded into the upholstery to keep it from slipping down.

Amazingly our cat was now almost 1.5 metres long! In this way, it was able to keep itself cool and relaxed as only a cat can do. Had he been lying on a coach, he would no doubt have reached two meters in length.

Our cat's posture reminded me of Dali's famous painting, *The Persistence of Memory*, where the clocks appear to be melting. Our cat's melting pose would have made Dali reach for his paint brushes in delight. No doubt

Salvador Dali, being Spanish, would also have appreciated that a siesta is a sensible way to make it through the heat of the day.

Nature and the seasons cannot be ignored. **The lesson was a simple one.** Instead of disconnecting, we can pay closer attention to the rhythm of nature and adapt to the moment. Instead of fretting about productivity, we can create more with better quality of work when we are comfortable and at peace.

If in doubt, ask your cat.

Chapter 5:

How Important is Drawing Actually?

Conventional wisdom goes that the ability to draw accurately is vital to becoming an accomplished artist. I speak here of the painter, not illustrator. This belief seems to stalk the beginner painter.

There was a time when young artists would spend their first year of training simply drawing with pencil and charcoal. Often these artists would become superb draftsmen and go onto producing fine realistic paintings.

But what if you prefer the painterly approach, often associated with the impressionist movement? My argument is that you need not be concerned about conventional drawing technique. There is a better way to train yourself.

Painterly painting seeks to capture the *essence* of a subject. It is not a photograph. It is rather a blend of emotion and technique that allows the viewer to fill in some of the content. How is this done?

The artist should avoid drawing in the conventional manner. That is taking a pencil and drawing an accurate outline of the subject. This is a common failing in the beginner's approach.

The next step will then be to fill in the spaces between the outlines. The artist may then think that it is a good painting, however, the artist will soon feel that something is missing - that element found in experienced artist's paintings that eludes the beginner. It is not quality of draftsmanship; it is simply due to a mistaken approach to painting.

On occasion, I have seen beginners paint watercolor in a free and easy manner. The resulting painting is often filled with basic shapes and has a fresh look. The same artist, when using oils, tends to labor the painting with fine brushes to get an accurate drawing. The end result is a stiff, formal and boring painting. How can the same person get such different results?

It comes down to **how the artist handles shapes.** A painting should be an exploration of bold shapes consisting of color notes placed next to each other. Just as great music requires notes placed alongside each other, **color notes, correctly placed as shapes,** will have a beautiful effect when viewed in totality.

Yes, this requires keen observation and it takes time to develop an eye for accurate shapes. To put it bluntly - **get the shapes and colors correctly placed and the drawing will take care of itself!**

The key to shapes is to forget about details. Think rather in terms of color masses. The V-like shape of a torso for instance - is it more rectangular? Look and then commit to the shape on the canvas.

A landscape, for instance, is often made up of four masses comprising light, dark and two mid-value shapes. The sky and tree line would be the extreme light and dark masses respectively. The distant hills, a mid-value as well as the foreground land, also being a mid-value. Far better to get these shapes and color masses down than to fret over drawing twigs and leaves!

These large masses can be refined with smaller shapes in warm or cool colors as you work from thin paint to thicker paint. Never get into the little brush details. The mind fills those in. A great way to ensure that masses remain your focus is to use a large brush.

It is surprising how a size 8 long, flat-bristle brush can be manipulated to produce many shapes. See how far you can get, then leave the painting. It will be finished.

While drawing should always be part of the artist's skill, it is not the determining factor in painterly painting. Shapes and color notes are the true objective.

Chapter Six

Reflections on a Modern Master

I am a lucky man! My wife purchased a copy of Kevin Macpherson's stunning book, *Reflections on a Pond,* as a birthday gift for me. Since the book had to be ordered from the US, there was much anxiety on her part waiting for its safe arrival in South Africa. Fortunately all went well and I am now the proud owner of a copy of this unique book, signed by the author, and endorsed with the following quote:

Every day is special brushed with the art spirit

I have been a big fan of Kevin Macpherson for many years. He is justifiably world renowned for his rich brushwork and meticulous color mixing that has made his paintings highly sought after.

Macpherson is also a leading exponent of the plein air movement. It is this part of Macpherson's process and works that had so intrigued me when I first came across his **online gallery**. Shapes and color, put down with brisk confidence in large dollops of paint, all coming together to show the essence of a fleeting moment. Intuitive painting that produces delightful impressions.

In the project, *Reflections on a Pond,* the artist set out to depict the pond on his New Mexico property on each day over a year. Set with a backdrop of stunning mountains and forest, the pond makes a perfect subject for this ambitious project.

Of course, the subject for any impressionist is the atmosphere and light. Having a reflective surface in the pond is a bonus that adds interest to the subject.

Macpherson used panels of 6x8" and a **basic palette of alizarin, cadmiun red, cadmium yellow, ultramarine and white**. Although each day of a year is depicted, for practical reasons the project took five years to complete. Over 500 panels were painted out of which 368 panels were selected for the book.

Imagine what all these panels would look like spread over your floor! Then, having to assess each one, record and photograph it for this coffee table-sized book. I can imagine that some artists may start a project like this and abandon it along the way. Kevin Macpherson saw it through, which speaks volumes about his dedication to his art.

The book is divided into four seasons, starting in winter. Several paintings per season have been printed in actual size. The photographs are sumptuous. The brushstroke's texture is clearly visible and the colors are gem-like.

The remainder of paintings are printed in smaller versions and dated in sequence. At the end of the book, **Macpherson's personal diary entries have been reproduced**. We are treated to an insight into his joys, frustrations and philosophy of painting.

He expressed interesting anecdotes. For example, the artist's displeasure with his neighbor for cutting down trees, the struggle to paint when energy is low, as well as the joys of a beautiful moment recorded in paint. All are faithfully recorded in his book.

A subtitle on page 15 reads: *"Magnificent Obsessions: From Monet's Garden to Macpherson's Pond"*. This series of work echoes Monet's obsession with light and atmosphere in his many paintings of the pond at Giverny.

Is Kevin Macpherson our contemporary Monet? I would certainly argue that he is a successor to Monet in the true sense of the artist's spirit.

I am also very grateful to have this book in my collection. It is unique and, needless to say, well worth adding to your library.

See the Official Website: Reflections On a Pond
See more of Kevin Macpherson's work here.

Chapter 7
The Rich Folk's Hoax
(The Artist's Distraction)

The other day I was caught up in the morning traffic. Since I do not usually have to be out in the "commuting cycle" I am always stressed about driving in the maddening rush. While waiting for a red light, I reached over and put the CD player on and listened to Rodriguez's album, *Cold Fact*.

While looking at the strings of glittering cars heading over the highways, off-ramps and on-ramps like part of an inhuman organism, I took note of the song playing on the CD. It was called *Rich Folk's Hoax*. Talk about perfect timing. The words were spot on and resonated with me in that moment.

Were we all chasing something that did not exist? Thousands of people charging off to work or to look for work seeking more. When is enough just enough?

"The poor create the rich hoax" sang Rodriguez. How true.

I know that we need to work and earn enough for the necessities of life. There is honor in that. I respect work. People that show up each day to support themselves and their families are the real heroes.

But the nagging thought that morning as I made my way through traffic was: is this the way to do it? This treadmill forced on us from the day we start school? Something is wrong with this system. How much time and effort goes into working for essentials and how much is devoted to foolish lifestyle expenses?

I wrote recently about the singer Rodriguez and his modest lifestyle. To call it extreme would be justified I think. But look at earlier times? Let's say our grandparent's days - the pre-consumer times when enough was just that, not more, more, more...

So we regular folks create the rich hoax and chase the pot of gold - even if it means using our credit cards to do it. College loans, store cards, bond extensions and easy payments.

What do you say? No more?

Chapter 8:

On Art, Love and War

Now I realise that the title of this post may suggest some philosophising is in the offing. That would be true. But indulge me.

I have been reading *Matterhorn* by Karl Marlantes. It is a brilliant novel based on the author's experiences in the Vietnam War. I know that this subject may not appeal to everyone, but it is an exceptional book.

The author, through his main character, considers the nature of humanity. I could not help but draw parallels with art. Why is art so important to the world? And more importantly, why do humans have a need to create art in the first place?

War is terrible and foolish. In extreme conflict, humans are capable of evil deeds which is one reason why wars are so awful. Being human, we are blessed with the ability to care - and cursed too. For us to perceive evil, we must be able to care and love first of all.

What if we were indifferent like other animals? Would there be wars? Apart from a scuffle over food or some other basic need, life would go on just fine. Hunting too would be an indifferent activity. Marlantes argues that it is our ability to care that brings us joy and misery.

Caring for others makes us human, but more importantly there is love. The Greeks understood that love came in different forms. The most important being *Philia* - love for your fellow human. *Love thy neighbour.* The least important to the Greeks was eros - love of the romantic kind that we modern westerners seem so besotted over.

What is the absence of love? Not hate, but indifference. Life can get along just fine in an indifferent world as animals and plants prove. Humans are a recent development in the grand scheme of the world, but love has turned us into something altogether different.

How does this relate to art? Well, if love is not essential for life on earth, then what about art? Why bother with art at all? Many school systems drop art altogether, especially in high school since it is viewed as unimportant. It is considered, at best, a luxury. But this does not make sense.

We create art because we are human. We also love because we are human. **To reject art or to be indifferent to art is to reject our humanity.**

Creating art is an act of love too. Love, for the process of creating and love for fellow humanity by sharing that art with others, is essential. It could be a painting or a designer chair, whatever. By creating art, we are respecting our highest emotional state - love.

When art is marginalized, I suggest we are doing ourselves and especially the youth a great disservice. It is one of the reasons why the media only equates love with sex. It is also a recipe for conflict, which the media cannot get enough of by the way.

Instead of cheapening love with the superficial and tawdry, let us look at what humans are capable of.

Creating art is something we can share with others and thereby demonstrate our love for our fellow humans. This has to be the message our children carry forward or we will see the same old cycles of destruction and prejudice.

Art and appreciation for art is critical. It is part of what makes us human.

Chapter 9:

Five Beliefs Artists Must Overcome

The beginning of the year is an interesting time. Interesting because we are all faced with a challenge. For our children this may be starting a new grade or college. For adults it seems that many are facing a financial challenge after the Christmas indulgence. Perhaps it is facing the same old job. These challenges teach us to persist. Without persistence we cannot get stronger.

From artists, I hear a lot of anguish over the economy. For some, the blame is internalised as they question their talent. Enough with the negative thoughts folks. **Here are five common negatives dismissed:**

1) **It is tough to survive on making art alone:** Yes, it can be, but this changes with time. We all know many others who have regular jobs with decent salaries yet are in constant fear of financial meltdown.

There is no guarantee that any job or profession will keep the wolf from the door. All that counts is our attitude. Do we push on through or give in to fear? It is a choice. There is no shame in moonlighting to get by. Do what must be done, but never give up on your art!

2) **Art is hard work. It would be easier to do something else:** If you really believe this then that is your reality. The truth is that any work we do for a living can get boring or difficult at times. Then it is up to us to shake it up a bit.

Recently I had some work done on our property. Watching the workers digging a trench in the summer heat made me appreciate once again how lucky I was. Would you want to trade places with those guys?

3) **My Talent has run out!** This is a common mental game we play with ourselves. When this self-pity crops up, we are wasting our time at that moment. We need to get to work!

We can only do one thing properly at any point in time. Take action and the doubts disappear. I recently watched the movie *Rush* about the Niki Lauda - James Hunt rivalry. Great movie. I am in awe of the tenacity of Niki Lauda. He never doubted his talent, but he was also logical too. When a course of action was needed he pursued it fully. When caution was required he adapted where necessary. It was not just about talent - it was all about **common sense and total self-belief.** Use both all the time.

4) **My Paintings are not what people want:** Says who? I am always amazed at the variety of art out there. Humans are capable of such amazing and transformational art. At the same time, it is frustrating that artists disempower themselves by relying on the droves of fickle critics for validation.

Sales too are not about whether one's art is good or bad. Sales is about selling. Either you are doing a good job at selling or not. If not, then study marketing and sales techniques.

5) **If only I ... (fill in the blank space):** Ever caught yourself saying these words? Maybe it was, "If only I landed a gallery deal, then my finances would be secure." Gallery owners would disagree on that by the way.

Maybe you secretly believe that, "If only I could paint like _____, then I would sell many more paintings." Not so fast. Well-known artists may sell paintings, but they have worked many years to get to that point. The art market is vast and can accommodate different price points and artists at various skill levels.

What counts is persistence and consistently learning about your work. Also remember to study the business of art. I believe that **the artist who follows this path will produce art worthy of a collector's attention.**

I hope that these self-defeating beliefs are not going to stalk you. Unfortunately some of these beliefs will always crop up when we let our guard down. Such is life. Try to laugh and carry on doing good work. All will be okay.

Painting's always a challenge. Sometimes my brush sings its wonderful song, sometimes I wade through quicksand, but always I persevere in gratitude.
(Julie Nilsson)

Chapter 10:

Wake Up and Live Your Art

When did you last feel inspired? The kind of inspiration that gets you out of bed and rushing off to try something new? It is easy to lose this spark until you notice it missing one day. That is the day you feel that time is leaving you behind. That is the time to take action. There is only now.

When I come out of these moments of sleepwalking and become aware of my day again, I realise that I only have a few moments in a day. Moments when I am free to create something new. To come up with ideas then put them into action. Most of my day is filled with busyness. Chasing chores and administration of some sort or another. Enough of that!

Simplify.
Turn off the phone. Put aside the social updates for a few hours. Switch off the TV and the absurd reality shows. Talk to someone face-to-face. Use your hands to make something. Breathe deeply.

Once the calmness returns, you will see how much you have to be grateful for.

I look at my walls and see the paintings. I dust off the frames. Take another look across the room and relive that moment. The moment when the idea for the painting emerged and took shape on my easel with so much ease. That is the moment of peace and renewal of energy.

I know that living without art is impossible.

Once art and the energy it brings is accepted into your life can you part with it? Here is to living with art. May it always continue.

Chapter 11:

Why Art? A Lesson from Mozart

It takes courage to purchase art. No matter the price. It is all relative anyway. To stump up with your money and say, "I want that painting," then to hand over your card, cash or click through the purchase takes a certain belief in something other than utility. Something bigger than a mere necessity.

What is the elusive quality that makes us stop and stare at a work of art? The great pieces compel us to look countless times and still we get something back. A buzz of pleasure, nostalgia perhaps or serenity. There is no begrudging the purchase then. What is obtained is a not merely tangible, it is simply more - and in this case more is good.

It is said that artists should know what their collectors want. Well let's say that in market-speak one should know what your customer wants or you will not have a clue what to sell. Does this apply to art? Should an artist ponder what collectors are looking for and trim and tuck the work to meet this belief? It is easy to answer in the affirmative, but what then? Creativity must run free.

Beauty is one of the rare things that do not lead to doubt of God. (Jean Anouilh)

I recently watched the movie Amadeus. You may remember this Oscar winning movie from 1984 about Mozart and his nemesis, Salieri. I saw the film back then, but wanted to see it again after all these years. It is still superb. Mozart is of course a genius and an artist in the true sense of the word.

Mozart was consumed by a passion for creating profoundly beautiful music. He was also driven to live life fully. Despite being surrounded by ugliness such as poverty and war, he sought out every opportunity to compose music and to live his life with joy. Did his music solve the problems of the day? Did his music boost the economy and lead to peace in Europe? No.

What about becoming rich? Money was never Mozart's motivation. Music was his purpose and he shared his gift wholeheartedly.

How does this help us understand what collectors want from art? I suspect that it comes down to beauty and escape. The more we are confronted by a world gone mad, the more we need to be reminded of its beauty, creativity and the human potential for good. Art is part of the evidence that humans can do good work. Collectors share this communion with artists.

So what is art good for? For reminding us that creating something beautiful is a divine gift that must be shared with the world. It takes courage and understanding to acknowledge this. Only fear and ignorance can stop us.

Chapter 12:
Plein Air or Studio?

Painting in the studio and painting outdoors. What is better? A silly question really, because they are both so different. Chalk and cheese, although I could argue that it is not so daft. What about the artist (myself included) who has some expectation that the next painting may be good enough to actually sell? That it will bring in some cashflow for those paints and other tiresome things like bills to pay? If plein air painting is hit and miss compared to the controlled environment of a studio, then staying indoors to churn out studio work will pay the rent. Or will it?

Remember exams at school? Some kids were great in class, but come exams they would fall apart. They could not handle the pressure and scrape tests that were easy to others. Then there were those who were useless on a daily basis, but then do rather well at test time. They turned out to be steady under pressure and did enough to get a respectable C. It is the kids who can handle pressure that make a success of life. The show pony's end up looking rather ordinary since life tends to be a pressure situation.

Now that all sounds a bit hard actually, but look at it this way: What if you can face the pressure situations, learn from them, and then apply the lessons learnt to do some excellent work when the pressure is off? That must surely be the way to live life too. Take it in your stride with some confidence and a smile. It is rather like how I view plein air painting.

The success ratio for plein air, if I think of saleable work, is about 50%. However, take that experience into the studio and it results in more authentic paintings more often. Turn the ordinary into the extraordinary. If you can paint the ugly and make it look interesting - worthy of consideration, then you have skill as a painter. Anyone can paint pretty, but pretty gets boring very quickly. Make the average beautiful. That is something.

I think of plein air as the training that gives me the endurance to solve painting problems quickly, to make decisions, and to get on with finishing the painting. Sometimes the conditions are not perfect. For example windy conditions, sun in your eyes and sunlight glare off the sea. Chances of a great painting - poor. So why bother?

The answer is that **the challenge is the attraction.** You know that success is unlikely, but you have an opportunity to learn to paint the sea's colors as you observe them. There is no contrived mixes of green and blue. What colour is the sea water in those conditions? Can you put a name to it? Not at all, but it is there so come up with a solution. Then there is the emotional content. How does that moment feel?

So in the end it is not a contest at all. Plein air is necessary to build the muscle for the long haul in the studio. Besides, it is great fun too!

Chapter 13:
These Two Things Give Paintings Maximum Impact

To see like an artist is the goal. There are two sides to this; the natural response and one we learn. The natural response is emotional and intuitive. Artists need to respond and paint emotionally. The response that we learn is through technique and practice.

One part of technique that adds the punch to a painting is how we see and paint shapes. The second is the relationship between light and dark values. Sounds like life actually.

Shapes can simplify the complex into something that we can better understand. We humans understand and respond to strong uncomplicated shapes. Maybe it is hardwired into us from evolution. After all, recognising a shape and responding to it quickly could save lives.

These days we respond to advertising and other signage because of simplified or stylised shapes. Add to this a **strong light/dark contrast in values** and we are drawn to the shape instinctively, so it makes sense to use this idea in painting too. Caravaggio understood this with his powerful use of light and dark contrasts.

Paul Cezanne pushed the idea of shapes to the point where perspective was almost broken. He simplified a vast landscape into a series of shapes devoid of detail, but still suggesting what was there for the viewer's mind to fill in.

Without adapting reality through shapes and values, an opportunity is lost to create something different – the ability to bring in the artist's emotional content that will excite the viewer's imagination.

How to paint with more impact and emotion? Look at powerful value contrast and simple strong shapes. What about colour? Yes, colour adds much to a painting, but take a look at black and white photographs and recognise the power of shapes and values. Think of Ansel Adams photos and the message is clear.

I have encouraged many art students to focus on painting studies using simplified shapes and strong values. The best way to start is to look for the big dominant mass shapes then draw them in black and white. This is also called a notan painting. From this simple exercise, the process of developing a strong painting can begin.

Here is a short video extract from my course, Learn To Paint With Impact, demonstrating how to use this technique. Try it yourself.

Chapter 14:

The Obsessive Artist

What image does the word obsessive conjure up in your mind? A negative one I should imagine. Perhaps even behavior that needs some professional help? Obsessive behavior can suggest extreme conduct that has negative consequences.

There is, however, a good side to obsessive behavior. There is scope for all of us to be a bit more obsessive about our passions. Artists can take note that being obsessive is a good thing and should be encouraged. Not sure? Take a leaf out of the book of science!

Recently I watched an excellent documentary on BBC called *In Search of Science* hosted by Professor Brian Cox. You may have seen it although I do admit that I came across it by chance. It was all about scientists that have contributed to our knowledge about the natural world.

The show started with a look at Sir Isaac Newton. That giant of a genius who amazingly was born in 1642! They were still burning witches back then and here was this man with a modern intellect simply centuries before his time.

Newton was obsessive about observing the natural world and finding solutions to problems. This was a good thing since his natural laws, proven by him through extensive experimentation, changed the world of science forever.

45

There were examples of other **incredible achievements by obsessive scientists**. All very well I thought. These boffins lived a long time ago. But then a mathematician came on who is currently working on one of the most perplexing problems: Finding an answer as to why the universe exists at all. Not only that, but being able to prove it mathematically.

What makes a genius? According to this mathematician, the drive to focus and solve a problem long after others would give up distinguishes many geniuses from the rest of us. Ten years of work is required to claim some sort of mastery on any topic. So a genius, or more correctly a master, has **an insatiable curiosity and drive** to solve the problems of whatever interests him or her.

It was argued that for most people, especially in this age of distraction, there is only a superficial interest in anything. We tend to gloss over topics. Nobody gets stuck in to master something anymore. Does this ring true?

Faced with a question? Just google it and you can get away with most anything it seems. But if you are designing a jumbo jet, then we would hope that there is a bit more work going into the project.

Should artists not also become obsessive about their art? Imagine if we could acquire the skill and knowledge of artists that we admire simply by working hard at our art. Does that seem like a good bargain? So what if it is a ten-year-plus deal? Many others may argue that it is a waste of time; that all the effort to master something like art will never keep the wallet fat. What about those scientists who plugged away without reward or recognition until late in their lives, perhaps to be vindicated years after their passing? Were they misguided?

Take Paul Cezanne and Claude Monet for example - two artists who persisted and struggled against popular opinion until they were acknowledged as titans of art in their later life. What if they were not obsessive?

The answer is that your life's purpose is at stake. There is no escaping this. What brings joy to the artist is art. To ignore it will bring regret. To accept your purpose will bring peace. Money is not the purpose, but there will be enough of it attracted to cover your needs and some luxuries too.

It seems that **if our purpose in life is at stake, then we should be obsessive about it**. We should work at our tasks, solve problems, grow in knowledge and always seek the next question so that we may answer it emphatically. The artist need not be embarrassed about it or apologise if the chores are delayed.

Obsess a little. Create a lot.

Chapter 15:

Your Art is Noticed

When you are striving to grow your artist's career it is easy to become disillusioned. Often your work, held so close to your heart, is met with indifference by the public or a few likes online - then silence. When will your art be noticed and appreciated?

At times like this it is worth remembering that you are not alone. Keep this in mind:

If no one is watching you perform or admiring your sculpture or displaying your painting or even reading your literary work, do not despair. You are not being ignored. Your art is noticed by God since it is God that gave you the compulsion to create. By taking action to create you are giving honour to God and the gift you have been blessed with.

That is enough for now. Tomorrow is another day.

Chapter 16: Must Artists Sell Out to Make Better Art?

In ancient times artists produced work for the good of their tribe or village community. Art was a gift not a commercial transaction. Art had a magical or ceremonial function, or was created simply to honor the heritage of the community. It was given and accepted freely.

This function of the artist continued in similar form for centuries. As commerce grew and a few wealthy community leaders arose, they could give patronage to a few artists. Of course, as monarchies and city states developed, so too did patronage.

However, things changed rapidly as the rise of the merchant class accelerated in the latter half of the eighteenth century. Add industrialisation to the mix from the1800s, and we see a complete change to modern lifestyles. A paradigm shift as the economists would call it.

More artists could take up the calling to create, but this increased competition and art as a gift was no longer viable. **Artists had to live and compete for a living just like members of other trades and professions**.

Artists still wanted to create unique work - different work that spoke for them, that would convey a message or concept that the artist needed to communicate. How could such risky work ensure an income?

After all the world had gone in the direction of mechanisation to meet demand for products. Cookie cutter art anyone?

Artists have a few choices.

First option: Work for the man and retire, then take up art.

Second option: Do art on the side while working at a regular job to pay the rent. Both of these options are compromises and will get in the way of creativity. This is not a criticism of either choice. You have to do what you believe is right for you - so long as you recognize the facts.

Third option: Do art fulltime and risk it all. This may work for a few, but there will usually be some sort of financial cushion to pave the way. Paul Gauguin, for example, relied on his former earnings as a stock broker. The odds will always be against the artist starting out. Wait for a state grant? Better get comfortable. It will be a long wait.

There is another option however. To sell out.

Selling out has been vilified as a betrayal of artist's principles. This idea is perhaps carried over from the sixties and seventies when counter-culture demanded that artists reject collar and ties and all that regimented mainstream thinking.

Artists working in corporations were simply regarded as suits. There was no art in such an environment. Time marches on and so too does the demands of the economy. Can artists compromise and still produce unique art?

The starving artists in tie-dyed T-shirts is a thing of the past. It seems that artists have moved into business and embrace selling out. There is precedent for this and it may surprise you to note that a leading exponent of selling out was Jim Henson of Sesame Street and Muppets fame.

In her book, *Make Art Make Money: Lessons From Jim Henson on Fueling your Creative Career*, Elizabeth Hyde Stevens illustrates how Jim Henson realised that money had to be obtained to make more great art. To produce, Sesame Street required cash.

Freedom to make art means not having to fret about paying the bills. Henson was encouraged to license Sesame Street toys, which was a move he hated to do, but with fantastic financial rewards that could be reinvested in his art. Henson realised that selling out with a plan and purpose was, in fact, giving him the **freedom to create unique art on his own terms**.

How does this translate for artists trying to make ends meet? What products can you produce that can be replicated in volume in order to raise funds for something unique? Perhaps prints, licensing, DVD's, books, downloads, lessons, demonstrations, freelancing and many other avenues opening up in the connected economy. All of these opportunities are part of the artist's way to fuel unique art.

It is the artist's unique art that is the modern gift. No, it is not given for free, but it is still created and shared in an age of commoditization. That is the gift. Without unique work our community is lost in sameness. If it means selling out to do so, then so be it.

Chapter 17:
Art, Belief and Magic

Is seeing believing? Is magic, by its very nature, an illusion? If so, how important is magic in our society today?

In art, when you believe what you see, then you allow the magic to happen. Without magic life would be rather boring for everyone. We humans love to be delighted by magic, even when we know it is an illusion. It is one of our unique traits, just like creating art is uniquely human.

We know the phrase, "to see like an artist," and we know that it applies to the technical things like seeing the shapes and values in a scene. It is much more than technique though. What is often overlooked is that the artist must see what will create the magic for the viewer.

The illusionist relies on sleight of hand to fool the audience. We believe and call it magic. The unexplained takes on a mystery of its own and it enthralls us. Yes, we know it is a trick, but we accept the bargain because of what we get in return. A moment of joy, wonder and escape. Is this not what we also get from art that moves us?

How does the artist make us believe? Take for example a painting by Turner called *Rain, Steam and Speed, The Great Western Railway*. A scene filled with light, wonder and mystery. In reality, it is a train charging across a bridge at the height on England's industrial revolution, spewing smoke and shrieking noise in a grimy industrial setting. We would usually hasten away from this awful reality, but the artist has seen something else.

Using his mastery of the medium, Turner has created a painting that makes us stare at it in wonder. We try to fathom what is going on and look for other details. Our minds seek out images as we peer into the golden mist and smoke. What is bearing down upon us? Our mind says it is a train, but our imaginations see a fiery maw charging towards us. Magic.

The painting hooks us in. Why? Deep down, we are part of a shared experience. At once repelled and also drawn in. There is more than our first impression of an everyday scene. There is something beautiful too. Would we see this without the magic of believing in the artist's work?

What would life be without these illusions that we accept so readily? Unacceptably dull and appallingly real. We all want the illusion - to escape and see beyond the material world, to believe in magic for a moment. That is true art.

Chapter 18:
Artists Never Retire, They Reinvent Themselves

Retirement. This word comes with many emotionally charged ideas. Mostly negative. For my father's generation, retirement was the reward that came after a long working life. If you were lucky, the company pension plan would kick in at age 65. If not, you had to rely on what little you had saved and the government pension would take care of you. This concept of retirement has not survived as long as those still believing in it. It is deader than roadkill.

Today we know that retirement is still a goal for the working masses - a time when we can relax and play with our grandchildren. Except we have had to plan for retirement with private retirement policies and savings. Not much of change from my dad's days, but more empowering for sure. More scary too, if you haven't built up a decent nest egg over twenty or more years. This idea of retirement also needs to be put to sleep.

Forget retirement. It is a word best suited to appliances, old cars and farm animals that are put out to pasture. Instead, let us consider another idea. Instead of retiring, we need to reinvent ourselves. This process is not for our sixties either; reinvention is best undertaken many times over our lifetime. At least every five years, maybe more, beginning from when we leave school.

What is reinvention all about? For starters if you have been an adult for some time, let's say you're in your forties, then you have probably reinvented yourself many times already. Perhaps you've reinvented yourself by a change in job, career, marriage, children, clothing or in many other ways in order to survive and thrive. The trick is to recognise these changes and use them for a process of mental change too. To put it bluntly, **sometimes we need to catch a wake-up!** Do ourselves a favour and live life. Stop moaning and blaming others and get on with it.

How to do this? Many ways beckon and opportunities abound if we look for them. Continuing education is critical. Learn skills. Read. Listen to podcasts and audio books. Try out ways to expand your mind and horizons. Each time we do this we are reinventing ourselves. It is a process of empowerment. It gives us Freedom from established dogma.

Reinvention in our sixties? Do you know that the most affluent retirees have multiple income streams after retirement? 98% according to figures from insurance giant Sanlam. In my dad's day, the idea of income streams in retirement, other than pension, was laughable. It was a sign that you have failed to carry out the masterplan. Today we understand that keeping our minds active with work that we love and choose to do is the key to fulfillment. Sure, you need a financial cushion in place for peace of mind, but you can now remain part of the economy, contribute and share in ways that were unthinkable twenty years ago.

Why the emphasis on artists? 'Artists' refers to anyone thinking and acting creatively. **Artists take responsibility for themselves and take action**.

Reinvention is the way for all artists of the world. How would you like to reinvent your day, week or year ahead? After all, it is your decision.

Chapter 19
Artist or Regular Job?
How to Make Tough Choices

How to make a hard choice? Imagine you have a child finishing high school. Your child announces that he has considered several career options and has narrowed it down to artist or attorney. As a parent what is your first reaction?

When I reached this milestone in my life, a career in arts meant something more industrial like textile design or even fashion design. A fine arts career was an oxymoron since everyone knew that outside of the education department there was no such thing as a career for fine artists. It was a life of struggle and desperation, simple as that. It is law my son and that is that.

Thirty years later, the world has become more enlightened. A degree is so generic that it seems almost pointless unless it is for a specific profession like medicine or engineering.

Yet **a decision between arts and traditional trades and professions is still a hard choice,** especially in "these tough times." So how does one choose in these circumstances? Philosopher **Ruth Chang on TED Talks** puts forward an empowering argument:

Consider the artist or attorney decision. Why do so many people opt for law instead of art? Because the fear of the unknown makes law seem like a less risky option. At least with law there is a prospect of earning more plus the social cachet of being a lawyer.

Those TV programs glamorising lawyers also help a lot. I confess that in my day the TV series *LA Law* was a hoot. But to base this decision on these criteria - fear and reward for example - is a mistake. You cannot hammer a round peg through a square hole without it ending in tears.

I can assure you that there are many young lawyers without work. Many others have had to start their own practice only to find that business is based on cashflow and the bank manager does not care what certificate hangs on your wall. No positive cashflow, no mercy.

Many young lawyers have had to close up shop deep in debt. Of those that have reasonably lucrative careers in law, there are many who yearn to be doing something else more creative. To make it in the legal business, like any other business, requires hard work, hustle and many years of dedication. The professional liability risks are huge though.

To succeed as an artist you will need the same dedication to the task. If you put in the work the rewards will come.

Perhaps the biggest downfall for artists is the idea that the world is out to get you – it is full of philistines who do not know great art from their elbow. "Oh, what is the use?" they say... Sorry, the world owes nobody any special favours.

What we see then is that a law career and an arts career are on a par. Both can work out and both can implode.

How to choose between careers that are on a par? Will more income sway you? Let's say you love art, but you can expect to earn 25% more as a lawyer. Will that make you choose law even if it makes you miserable? It is unlikely that money alone will make the difference.

Chang argues that in a hard choice situation **you have the power to make your own reasons.** What are your unique qualities and how do they fit in with the career. If you love art, but are lukewarm on a law career then it is likely that your law career will collapse in the near future.

If your joy and happiness are focused on art then it is more likely that art will sustain you. **You have the power to be the author of your own life**. Your subjective reasons are valid.

How to make this hard choice in mid-life? The fear of losing what you have accumulated now kicks in. Suddenly your assets and things that were the goal before become the shackles that bind you.

The decision should be easier if you have a financial cushion to absorb a career change. Sadly this is seldom the case. **Fear increases with age**. There is also a sense of noble martyrdom that keeps many professionals slogging on with work they hate. Sacrifice for a noble cause. Bitterness and regret beckon.

Just maybe our loved ones would rather have a happy mom, dad and spouse at home? It is a thought. Perhaps we can face these hard decisions more clearly and make the correct choice for ourselves?

Chapter 20
Spontaneous Hard Work Delivers Better Results

*Do not bc afraid that too much labour
over the composition is going to kill the
spontaneity. Those who absorb and digest
their experiences are, of a sudden,
mountains of strength and can produce
pictures of spontaneous start and finish.*
(John F Carlson)

That old nemesis of mine has stopped by my studio this week. Perhaps it is because I have had a busy few weeks on commissions, which had led me to lower my guard? This old friend, or should I say fiend, disguises itself in many inviting ways. Before I knew it, time had gone and I had nothing to show for it. I speak of *procrastination.* That *artist's bane* if I want to get all "middle earth" and dramatic.

I have no shortage of ideas for new projects and I have a list to prove it. Yes there is much to do, but... Then I came across the above quote by American artist John F Carlson. A renowned landscape artist of the early 20th century and art mentor.

There is the notion that we must paint every day to become anywhere near good enough to make it. Well there is much to say about that idea and the debate could go on. I know that I held to that notion as well, but not anymore.

I do believe that an artist must paint often and as much as possible, but there must be a foundation first; a foundation of study, thought and preparation. If this means taking time off to think on a subject, then do so. To spend a few days sketching, tinkering with color mixes perhaps and then? Action!

Spontaneous action that has focus and intent will achieve much more in a day than aimless repetition over six weeks.

I particularly love the part where Carlson says "Those who absorb and digest their experiences..." Is that not what being an artist is all about? Writers do their best work when they rely upon their close observations of life and past experiences. Artists who paint simply to record without relying upon their experience will render a painting lacking in emotion.

Mountains of strength... **Wow!** No simpering little brush fiddling about here! Paint with strength and energy. Large brushes, much paint, bold color and strong values. That will do far more for creating a painting with impact than days of overworking in the studio.

Spontaneous work can mean diving in and completing a painting *alla prima* or it can mean approaching the painting session with gusto on day two. The point is to get stuck in and try to let intuition guide you. You have prepared for the game, but you cannot ignore its natural flow. Go with it.

Often you will find yourself breathless at the end of a painting session. Your arm may be tired and you will feel mentally spent. Is that not living fully in the moment?

In the end it is about a balance between preparation and completion. Both are part of the artist's life and all are connected to produce a worthy painting. It is an attitude that we can all access if we want it. It will not take the fun out of painting or add pressure to produce.

I am willing to bet that Carlson's approach of labor and spontaneous action will add excitement and fulfillment to your painting experience.

Chapter 21

Art Demands Courage from the Artist

For Above all else, beyond imagination and skill, what the world asks of you is courage to risk rejection, ridicule and failure. (Robert McKee)

It seems that every day I need to call on courage to do work on my art, share it and let it go. Courage comes prepacked in the young and appears to diminish over time. Why is that?

Sometimes one has to wonder why we still stump up to the easel, keyboard or whatever workstation you have to plug away. It takes courage to show up and do the work.

But then who can complain when one has another chance to make good? That is the crux I think. Today could be a breakthrough moment. Hope.

It is that bit of excitement at the possibility of doing something special. It opens the curtain to the soul and the light pours in. Create something and risk be damned!

Chapter 22

SHOCKER! This is Why Collectors Buy Art

Please excuse the tabloid headline. I could not resist. The world of high-end art collecting is vulgar at best these days. Oligarchs and other scandalously wealthy continue to flex their wallets and egos to purchase art for ridiculous sums. To add further insult many of these works remain hidden in vaults when they should be on display. Perhaps a fake version is displayed for guests while the original is stashed away for safety?

However, all is not lost for us common folk. While the billionaires buy art for their egos, status or investment, there is a growing trend for collectors to buy art for the simple reason that they like it. That was the "shocking" news in a New York Times article titled, "Banking on the Appeal of "Bad Art".

Collectors are comfortable buying art that is recognizable and uplifting; also at prices that will not threaten their children's inheritance.

If you like to purchase original art at affordable prices, then this news may seem silly. However, for galleries that are struggling in these recessionary times, this may be good news indeed. Art that is accessible, such as art in an impressionist style, can sell for good prices for both collector and gallery.

It is OK to have art that is beautiful for the sake of beauty. You no longer have to grit your teeth at shock art, for instance, to impress your peers. Political art is one thing, but to grace your home? Perhaps not.

If you are wondering about the quality of this art, then rest assured. A **high price does not guarantee good quality**. Affordably-priced art can be of the highest quality. Most artists are using top quality materials and do take their art very seriously.

Any professional artist today will have to strive to produce excellent quality art to survive. High prices at auction has much more to do with provenance. Who owned the art work can hugely inflate auction prices.

The recent BBC documentary, *What Makes Art Valuable?* provides a fascinating look into the high-end art market. Watch the *documentary* and be amazed by the prices and motivations behind the purchases of the top ten most expensive paintings.

No doubt there will always be super wealthy collectors making up headline prices, but is there a change in sight? **Will art be simply about art again?** No price tags taking centre stage, but simply for the transcendence that art brings to artists and collectors alike?

It is revealing that many art dealers and collectors in the above documentary rue the outrageous prices. Do these prices have any relationship to the art itself? You decide.

Collecting art is fun and I have never regretted purchasing a beautiful painting. I look at these paintings on a daily basis. It is a moment of peace that I am grateful for. I would not like to worry about market prices and insurance. That was not the artist's intention and it would surely ruin the experience.

Chapter 23

Do the Work! Lessons from Van Gogh

The first attempts are absolutely unbearable.
I say this because I want you to know that if you see
something worthwhile in what I am doing,
It is not by accident but because of real direction
and purpose. (Vincent Van Gogh)

In this time of media and information overload it is easy for artists to get caught up in the whole tussle of marketing. This is understandable. The internet and all the possibilities that go with thousands of apps, social media and wireless connectivity compels us to try something. Not to do so seems almost negligent. Are we not supposed to improve our business skills in this new age? Must we not all be self-sufficient and productive?

Aside from a few celebrity artists who can live like recluses while their agents do all the messy marketing, we need to take charge and make things happen. Yes, I know that I have only seconds to get a collector's attention when there are so many other artists offering their work online.

I know, rather vaguely, that websites must be optimized and this is called SEO. I expect that I will need a teenager to explain it all, but I shan't bother because there are better things to do. Like painting.

Running after sales can be time consuming and stressful. Vincent Van Gogh would no doubt agree. So Vincent left this job to his brother Theo, which was not the best move in art marketing history.

Yes it is stressful and I find that this hampers my work. Painting is, for me, an emotional thing, not technical.

Of course, there are many techniques in painting, but once I get an idea for a painting I go for it. It is an emotional process. My mood has a direct bearing on the painting. There is simply no getting away from it.

Van Gogh's quote above may seem to describe his process as a technical exercise. This is surely a mistake. He was rather talking about persistence. Van Gogh's work is seething with emotion. There is no doubt that Van Gogh, once he had an idea in mind, painted with furious attention. Every brushstroke is filled with vigour. His trees, for instance, would writhe like snakes on fire. The farm fields appear to be baking in the heat and the figures broken and bent under the relentless burdens of rural life.

Yes, Van Gogh knew how to work hard. He would make an early start each day and sometimes work until after nightfall. Pushing himself to extremes of mental and physical exertion was evidently the wrong way to go about it. Today, the experts would talk about keeping an optimal work-life-balance. Van Gogh had other problems to worry about as we well know.

The net result of Van Gogh's dedication is a body of work that is treasured to this day. Is there a more famous artist? There is even a **very good song** about him and we are all listening now.

What to take away from Van Gogh's process is:

- **Get started with your real work.** No procrastination.
- Approach your creative process with dedication and purpose
- Do your work as best you can to produce better work over time
- Do not be distracted by the grandiose promises of the internet and media noise;
- Make your own way, but do not be a recluse either,

- Moderation in all things. This is fun so make time for it.
- **Persist**
- Do not ignore your loved ones. They make it all worthwhile.

Make a start and produce something worthwhile. Start again. That is what artists must do before anything else.

Chapter 24

An Artlst's Sacred Space

Every artist needs a space to make art. Fortunate artists have a dedicated space they call their studio. Others have to make do with a corner of the living room or bedroom. The latter aspire to greater things as I did once when I used my bedroom corner as an improvised studio. I did not mind and it trained me to be careful about messing paint. A useful skill. Now I have a suitable studio all to myself. How fortunate I am.

There is no doubt that the word studio conjures up romantic images. It certainly sounds a lot better than *office*. Spending time in your studio sounds like time well spent.

"Oh, I was just in the studio working on a new piece" sounds quite posh and sophisticated.

On the other hand does anyone wish to spend more time in an office? Why would they? It sounds too much like unpleasant work.

Setting up a studio is not difficult. An easel and a small side table for your palette and paints is sufficient. A little cupboard space to keep some of the other items like brushes, jars, painting panels and so forth will ensure a neat and welcoming spot.

The most important point is that your space be ready for more work at short notice. I was looking at a photo of Paul Cezanne's studio. Google it if you have a moment. It is well preserved and cared for. Beautiful grand window panes allow light in on one side. The walls are painted a greenish wash that is soothing to the nerves. There is real energy and sacred calm within such a space. I hope to visit it one day.

Aside from having your studio on standby for when the muse strikes, one will also need to keep an eye on creeping clutter. This condition befalls all artists. I sometimes open the studio door to stare at piles of assorted artist's kit blocking free movement and wonder where it all came from.

Clutter is insidious. It robs energy and hampers free thought. There is another problem however; artists seldom spot the clutter before it reaches critical conditions.

Fortunately I have my wife who is the bane of all clutter. She recently put me on notice to sort out my studio. **This might have turned into a domestic disturbance**, but I had to concede that I could not reach into certain corners without moving piles of canvasses, used paint tubes and other oddments that should have been binned long ago. I had to do something.

So a Saturday was set aside for the task. What I thought would be a morning's work turned into two days of labor that left me with aches and pains for the next week.

My better half made me carry out every item in the studio until we had the bare shell. The walls needed repainting and from there it was an extreme makeover. Nothing was spared and we were ruthless.

How did a converted garage turn into a cluttered studio? Give it a few years and other priorities. Before you know it you have something that will no longer be an energising space within which to create. Having gone through this process I am resolved never to repeat it. If something comes in, then another item must be thrown out.*

I know there are some artists who seem to insist on cluttered studios, but I suspect they are missing out on something. A studio must be a sacred space where energy can move freely. Air, light and sound, not to mention the artist's movements, must never be blocked by clutter. Friends and collectors should not be horrified by noises and movement under piles of canvasses. Rather let them share your studio and the delight you have in creating.

So, if you have a studio, take a moment to assess whether it needs a clean out. You may remove a few creative blocks together with all the clutter. Have fun!

I will of course break this resolution and repeat the process ad infinitum.

Chapter 25

The Artist Who Conquered Doubt

When making a painting only one
thing counts: What you do next.
(Darby Bannard)

It is one of the peculiar parts of human nature. The desire to create something as well as the appreciation of art for art's sake. No other species does this.

What makes this even more peculiar is that art is perceived as merely a luxury. True, when survival is at stake, purchasing or creating a painting is not a priority. Yet even in the extremes of war, the preservation of art was important. Important enough for people to risk their lives. We saw this in the true story depicted in the movie *Monuments Men*.

Think of the history of art. What compelled cave paintings when life was so precarious? Perhaps art had supernatural power to help them survive? Despite weapons and strength, the human mind sought something more from art.

Even in these modern times, art can provoke extreme responses. But how is this relevant to you and me? I simply want to make art and maybe you feel the same or you want to collect a special piece of art.

There is still one big issue that artists struggle with. It is the lingering doubt that what they are producing is not good enough. Even worse is the artist who does not start creating because of self-doubt.

Yes there are other challenges artists face too, but, so long as the doubt exists, there is no more energy to face these challenges. That is what doubt does. It steals the artist's will to create. What is the answer?

There is only one response to doubt. Make a start. Persist.

We would not have been given the urge to create and appreciate art if it was not important. Animals can attack and destroy and so too can humans. But only humans create art for the sake of art. It does matter.

Art is part of what makes us unique, so when the doubts surface remember that your art is necessary. Do not hide your talents. Share your art and be confident that you are following a tradition of endeavor that is unique in the universe.

Chapter 26

Painting Commissions: Tips for Artists and Collectors

The words "I would like to commission a painting" should be exciting to any artist. It is a compliment and a financial windfall. However, commissions can go horribly wrong if the basics are not covered. Commissions are simply part of the artist's repertoire and come with their own unique challenges.

Here are a list of considerations for both artists and collectors:

Artists:

1. **Do not be guided in your decision by money alone.** Despite having the wolf camping outside your door, it will not solve your problems if you accept a bad commission deal. You will only add to your troubles.

2. **A commission is a relationship with a collector.** It is not the trading of goods. The difference is huge and requires both parties to get to know each other. If this scares you then rather pass.

3. **Communication is key.** Ask the collector questions such as: the subject of the painting, what size the painting must be, where it will be displayed, framing requirements, which of your current works the collectors likes most. Also ask what the collector does not want. These will all give an indication of what the collector imagines your painting will look like. These basic questions will lead to more questions and clarity

4. **Personality Issues?** Much as I would like to keep it all business, it is not possible since painting has a strong emotional content for both parties. If there is a personality clash, the whole deal will end badly. This can have a major negative effect on the artist's morale. Keep your eyes open for these issues early on so that you can pass on the job if uncomfortable.

5. **Price:** This is often easily agreed upon, but needs to be sewn up properly. Put it in writing, even if it is only recorded in emails, with a written acceptance by the collector. Agree on price and a deposit (usually one-third up front non-refundable). Negotiate if you must, but know in advance where your sticking point is. Do not undervalue yourself. Keep costs such as materials, delivery, framing and your time in mind. You do not want this to become a financial loss.

6. **Progress:** I like to keep collectors updated on progress. I do not send photos until near completion and finally upon completion. If the collector can view it in person then do a reveal and make it a fun

occasion. It is at this point that you want to deliver and be paid in full too.

7. **Payment:** This is where things can get sticky. I suggest that delivery only take place once full payment is received. This is accepted practice, but you will find requests from collectors who want to take the painting on approval before making their mind up. Resist this as it can throw the entire deal into doubt. The painting is complete and you are entitled to full payment. Not payment in instalments. Be strong!

8. **Get Excited!** Talk, share and have fun. Your vision and the collector's vision are beautiful things to talk about. Keep the entire process an enriching experience for both of you.

Collectors:

1. **Be Realistic**: Unfortunately some art lovers are so moved by their favourite artist's work that they want a large painting or two. Both parties get caught up in the excitement of it all, but then price comes up and everything fizzles out. By having checked out the artist's other paintings and prices you will have an idea what the cost will be. Do some homework on this and it will help you negotiate without being embarrassed.

2. **Know What You Want:** Be prepared with the subject matter in mind. Reference photos in place and a good idea about size of the painting. Do not be shy about what you want painted and where it will be displayed. Yes we know that paintings need to match the decor sometimes. That is life.

3. **Price:** Without repeating myself be sure about the price and get this all confirmed in writing. Then stick to the deal.

4. **Progress:** Get an idea on duration of the project. Although things come up and there may be delays this should not add months to a project. Sometimes time is critical. Make this a point of the contract. Ask for updates, but do not nag the artist. Calls and texts every few hours will not help!

5. **Have You Commissioned Work Before?** Yes both artist and collector have track records. If you have commissioned art before then tell the artist. It will give the artist some comfort too.

6. **Share Your Vision:** If you are new to the art world, you may feel shy about opening up about your vision for the painting. Do not hold back. Artists should welcome your feelings as this will help them get into your psyche a bit. It will help with the painting as there is an emotional factor involved.

7. **Any Issues before delivery?** If there is a major issue with the completed project such as quality of work, materials or some departure from what was understood then try and resolve it amicably. Usually there is not a big issue at such a late stage because each party did their due diligence.

Commissions can be fun for artists and collectors. By taking a few common sense steps there should not be any problems, but rather the start of a beautiful relationship between artist and collector.

Chapter 27

The Joy of Pastel Painting

Pastels are often regarded as the poor cousins of oil painting and watercolours. No doubt those cheap and nasty pastels in the stationery store add to this idea. There are also much fewer pastel paintings on display than oils and watercolour. This has added to the perception that pastels are not equal to other media.

Pastels may however be making a strong comeback. They should and here is why:

1. Pastels are not a form of expensive chalk. Chalk is made with dye whereas artist's pastels are made with pure pigment held with a binder to give pastels there shape and workability.
2. The pastel colours are strong and vibrant due to their pigment content. Not weak as the word *pastel* may suggest to the uninformed.
3. Pastels are convenient to use anywhere.
4. The entry requirements for artists, as far as materials are concerned, are low.
5. Pastels, while not cheap, last a long time and give good value.
6. Pastels are exceptionally versatile (more on this later)
7. Pastels have been used by master artists for centuries. Consider master artists like Edgar de Gas and Toulouse Lautrec who created wonderful impressionist paintings and sketches with pastels.
8. Pastel paintings last well too. Provided they are framed behind glass they are not going to be disturbed and will not deteriorate.

The versatility of pastels is second to none. They can be used as a basic drawing medium. Pastels are handy to plan a painting as you can draw, establish values and settle colour plans before embarking on a painting.

Pastels can be **used as a painting medium** too as you can layer and mix pastel colours easily. The control of this mixing and placement of colour makes pastels ideal for loose impressionist work or highly rendered realism. You choose.

Additional variety can be obtained by using various forms of underpainting. For example underpainting in watercolour or diluted acrylics can create exciting effects to subsequent pastel layers. Alternatively the first layers of pastel can be mixed with a brush using water or artist's spirits. This is especially useful in establishing darks for later pastel layers.

Note that artist's pastels bear no resemblance to **cheap and nasty oil pastels** found in some stationery shops. The latter are simply oil crayons and are best avoided. Artist's pastels come in three main varieties - hard, medium and soft. The hard pastels can be used for underpainting or drawing the composition. Medium pastels and soft pastels will be used more often for the painting stage. Unison makes excellent medium pastels while Sennelier are famous for their soft pastels.

What about pastel paper? The main issues here are the tooth and tone of the paper. Tooth refers to the texture of the paper while tone is the color of the paper. The texture should not be too rough, but still have enough texture to hold layers of pastel. A fine portrait canvas will work too.

Pastel paper can be expensive so experiment with good water color paper. I have tried this to good effect. (See my YouTube channel for demo videos on this topic)

Try mounting watercolor paper onto board to get a painting panel similar to an oil painting panel. You can prime watercolor paper with gesso on the rear of the paper before sticking it to a board (MDF or similar good quality board).

This gives an excellent painting board that can be transported in a painting carrier outdoors. The paper will not buckle once framed either. I frame these boards without a matt board, but more on this my next article on framing pastels.

I also enjoy the fact that **I can paint outdoors in comfort with pastels**. Setting up is easy and there are no liquids to worry about. But make sure you can transport your finished painting in a panel carrier to protect the surface.

So give pastels a try. Oils are still my first love, but pastels are fast becoming a regular part of my painting process.

Chapter 28

Walter Mitty and the Artist Within

*The brave may not live
forever, but the cautious do not
live at all. (Meg Cabot)*

There is a bit of Walter Mitty within us all. That part of us that dreams of adventure, excitement, new directions and acknowledgement. Do you still daydream? I know, as a youngster, I was always in dreamland. The dreams became scarcer after I had to make a living in the real world. That is probably when most of us start to dream less year after year.

Walter Mitty however kept on dreaming as an adult. His creative soul kept pestering him while a safe life tried to keep him locked into a grey existence.

If you recall, the novel, *The Secret Life of Walter Mitty*, by James Thurber, is about an average guy leading a dull life, but who has rather intense daydreams. But in this instance, I am referring to the excellent movie remake starring Ben Stiller.

Walter, ironically working for Life Magazine, is in charge of the photography processing and archives department. Once again a world filled with art from the world's best photographers.

Walter gets to see these images and makes sure that they are printed in the magazine. Naturally his imagination is fueled by these images and he dreams of leading an exciting life which will also help him win the love of a beautiful woman.

Walter is finally propelled by a crisis at work to seek out a famous photographer. We get to see that the **universe is constantly placing opportunities before us** if we choose to look for them. It reminds me also of the Mission Impossible message that says "...your mission, should you choose to accept it..."

Walter finally chooses to accept his mission and take an opportunity, which leads to another and so it goes. Walter is finally living the life he once only dreamed about. Is it easy? No, it is hard work and not always safe, but that is never part of the equation. It comes down to accepting your life's potential or simply existing.

Walter Mitty has the soul of an artist. He deals with photographs and knows what a powerful image is. He knows what art is, but vicariously lives through other artists - until he chooses to live his own art; to create something unique and special with his own life. Is this not true for all of us?

If our lives are something we get to create through choices and action then we are creating something unique. Life does not require us to sacrifice ourselves to an idea. The myth of the office, promotions and retirement at 65. The idea that one way is the only way. Sacrifice to these ideas is not an authentic way to live.

We are misled by fear into these paths more than any other emotion. Of course we know that following a career out of fear is not a recipe for a fulfilling life. Neither is simply doing nothing. No, we are required to do the work that fulfills us. The question is what are you to do?

An artist will see opportunities and know what is required once fear is overcome. **That is** *the making of a brave man.*

Be brave and do your art.

Chapter 29
Britain's Greatest Artist: JMW Turner

Joseph Mallord William Turner (1775-1851) was an artist ahead of his time. By a long way. Looking at his paintings, one is tempted to say that he was an impressionist yet his work predated the impressionists. Turner took his own path and shocked the established artists with his extraordinary use of colour, texture and modern subject matter.

Turner's use of colour is both expressive and romantic, but not in the classical sense. He used colour in a way that would leave the viewer enthralled, moved and even shocked - never indifferent. No doubt, Turner did inspire impressionist painters who noted that Turner painted atmosphere and not simply objects. The air became the subject and this was a trait followed by many impressionist painters, most notably Claude Monet, who loved Turner's misty atmospheric paintings.

Take his painting, *The Slave Ship*, for an example. The painting depicts a true event where slaves are thrown overboard from a ship. Nature seems to be appalled by the deed. The red sky, tumult in the sea and the approaching typhoon all add up to a dramatic scene. The ship and the people are very small compared to the environment. Yet another statement about humans' arrogance and contempt in the eyes of our natural world. Clearly Turner felt that mankind's actions were an affront to nature.

In his painting, *Rain, Steam and Speed,* Turner depicts the symbol of industrialisation. The Steam Train as it ploughs through the atmosphere like an awful fire breathing creature. Industrialisation would change the landscape and our lives forever. Turner knew this and he was fascinated with the dramatic impact between past and present.

Notice the vigour of brushwork, layers of paint and unusual (for the time) paint techniques like scumbling. It is very modern for the time and would be at home in a contemporary gallery today.

Turner's influence would go further than the impressionists. His influence continues to this day and for this reason he is probably Britain's greatest painter.

Chapter 30
See Like an Artist: Notes on Paul Cezanne

I still recall parts of my high school art lesson on Paul Cezanne, especially the bit where Cezanne was preoccupied with reducing nature to three shapes: the cone, the sphere and the rectangle. I could not see the point of it at the time. Why not paint what was there?

Only much later did it dawn on me that that is exactly what Cezanne was doing, except Cezanne was able to see past the distractions and details. Everything was a shape falling within those three elements.

Cezanne went even further and attempted to depict each shape as a distinct colour. Not entirely flat colour, but the large simplified shape could be distinguished as a particular colour. We would recognize this effect as pixels in an enlarge photo, for example.

It may seem trite today, but not if you want to paint with understanding. To understand that nature, and by extension paintings of nature, can be simplified into basic shapes is to unlock the secret to painting. The truth.

Leave the details for the mind to fill in. After all our minds are constantly looking for work.

We must marvel at Cezanne's breakthrough and tenacity to follow this idea. Fortunately he was a stubborn fellow. It took guts to produce paintings like these instead of following what was popular.

What to paint? Cezanne showed us the question remains: What do you leave out? Everything but the shapes.

Take some time to look at Cezanne's paintings, particularly his landscapes and still life paintings, then consider a landscape scene in your area. Squint a little to reduce the details. Look for the light and dark mass shapes. Start with painting those and work from there. See where this direction leads you.

Chapter 31

Know Your Story

It helps to know why you are creating something. Simple as that sounds, I believe that being an artist is not just about mastering technique. You become an artist when you understand why you are creating something. Why the subject speaks to you. Then you can go ahead and develop that story.

It is OK not to know these answers when you are learning your trade. Ask the question nevertheless and let you unconscious mind chew on the answer. In fact this applies at all stages. **Keep asking why**.

The idea of telling a story has always been a part of visual art. In the past, this was fundamental to art. Consider the religious works of medieval art for example. Packed with symbolism, allegory and messages to educate, enthrall and sometimes terrify the viewers.

It was not only the Church that relied on art to tell a story. Royalty, and later the merchant classes, used paintings for political or social ends. In an age before widespread reading and our modern communication channels, paintings were vitally important story telling mediums.

Those days are gone yet story telling is still a powerful way to communicate ideas. It is our nature to use a story to understand a message.

Now we find our stories in so many formats. Indeed we suffer from story overload at times. Often it is enough to enjoy art for its beauty alone. Art for art's sake.

As an artist and writer I need to remember that story is important even in a simple landscape painting. Instead of just painting a scene, can I find something similar that has a human interest element? A story of some sort? Even adding a figure can make a simple scene so much more.

An example is a little plein air study I did at our local beach. There is a surfer who arrives each day (it seems) with several Border Collies. While the old surfer goes out to do his thing, the dogs roam free to explore the beach. It is a good life for the dogs I reckon.

I started this painting intending to paint the surfer and one of his dogs. Then I realised that I found the dogs to be the reason I was interested in the painting. The dogs were the story. So out went the surfer and the dog remained. Simple. The little painting was telling a story and not surprisingly someone who loves dogs and the beach purchased the painting.

Look for the story that appeals to you and see whether the spark of creative storytelling adds something to your enjoyment.

Chapter 32

How to Be a Plein Air Superhero

Yes it is a bit mad, but it is the silly season and almost time for the holidays. A bit of fun after a busy year never did anyone any harm right? For me this means family time and because it is summer for us in the southern hemisphere it is prime time for plein air painting.

Now I know that the idea of painting outdoors scares many artists out there. Is it safe? Will I make a mess and waste my time? The biggest worry is whether you will make a fool of yourself.

My answer to these are:
Yes it is safe with a little common sense.
Yes you may make a mess, but so what. How else do we learn? and finally -
No you are not making a fool of yourself. Plein air painting follows a long tradition of master artists getting outdoors to learn from the real world.

So how can you be a plein air superhero these holidays? By getting organised you set yourself up for success.

If you are travelling away for a few weeks and want to make sure that you have your studio essentials then try my **Studio-in-a-Box** © set-up. I have used a metal toolbox with drawers that holds more than enough oil paints, pastels and watercolor for a few weeks, plus other studio items like gesso, spirits, tape, brushes, palette knives, paper towel and medium all fit in safely.

This is a heavy box once filled up, but takes up very little space. It is not for lugging to the beach, but rather to set up your base at your holiday destination.

For an easel there is no better kit than a **pochade box**. This painting box that fits onto a tripod will make your life much easier. You can even do away with the tripod and simply put the box on your lap, but ideally you want to move back and forth regularly to see the painting clearly.

Of course there are the larger easels like the French box easels and more expensive aluminium ones. However, travel as light as possible for a pain free painting day and save the money for other fun activities!

For more **portable travel arrangements,** a converted suitcase backpack will do the trick. This bag takes my pochade box and tripod plus all the paints and brushes I require plus many other little items. If it is on wheels so much the better.

I can take this bag anywhere and set up whether on the beach or in the countryside.

Additional items could include a large umbrella especially for beach painting. Sunscreen, hat and water. A container that can be sealed for solvents and other painting waste for safe disposal later is essential.

A wet **panel carrier** makes life easier for transporting oil paintings back home. You can also use spacers between panels and then secure the panels with elastic bands with the dry surface facing outwards. Some painters simply use a few match sticks glued onto the rear of the panel's edges for this purpose.

Where to paint if you are nervous about your first efforts in public? Start in your backyard or balcony. Get the hang of this experience so that you at least have a sense of what you are dealing with. You can also test out your kit. Practice setting up your easel and how you will lay out your paints. All of this helps with your confidence.

Remember that Claude Monet painted extensively in his garden. He even painted many great works from his hotel balcony in Paris. All of this counts as plein air as you are painting from real life in the open air.

If you want a little more inspiration I do have a course specifically for new plein air painters called Learn Outdoor Painting with Confidence.

Have fun painting wherever you go these holidays!

Chapter 33

When Your Overthink it, You Lose the Essence of It

How to express yourself as an artist? What is your message? Have you done justice to the subject? What if you are making a fool of yourself?

These questions and many more stalk every artist. It is no little thing to put your work before others with not a care for the reaction. In truth it is an achievement to get that far. Many do not even begin to create their art. The hurdle of doubt is too high.

The saying goes that if you think it then it already exists. If you do not believe you can paint then that is so. You will not paint. If you stall at the point of starting and quit then you will never know. Could the work really be beyond you?

I hear it from many artists who struggle to get started. No time, no talent, no support, no space, and on it goes... These are serious thoughts that must be faced like the school yard bully. Not to means defeat and regret.

This is no way to live. Face the thoughts - shine light upon them and see them for what they are. Fearful ideas that pretend to be real and scary, but like the bully, are sent scampering when called out.

97

Take action today!

If you want to paint then begin this weekend with these **three action steps:**

1. **Find a spot to set up your easel** so that you see it ready and waiting. Try to use a place where you can leave the easel so that it is easy to resume painting. This is important.
2. **Use what you have.** Try not to worry about having the best materials. The basics like a brush, the primary colours and white and a canvas will be enough to start. If you have more than this then you are more than ready.
3. **Learn as you go.** Yes self-doubt will encourage you to wait for a workshop with your favourite artist. No matter how long it takes. Rather start now. You can take an online course in the evening and paint in the morning. Or pause the course and paint. So Begin!

There it is. No complication or overthinking required. Only good old-fashioned work and a can-do spirit.

You can let me know how it goes if you like. I am always happy to hear from artists.

Chapter 34

Have Fun Today Painting the Clouds

Skies and clouds - beautiful to look at when we have a moment. We often have our head down reading or looking at something and miss so much that is going on above us. The sky has fascinated humans since the beginning. For artists, the sky is the source of constantly changing subject matter and light. What would we do without light!

The sky should be considered like any other subject that you can paint. **The biggest issue** though is how do you paint something that changes so rapidly? Would it not be best to simply take a photo and paint what you see there - frozen on paper or the monitor? This can certainly work depending on your painting concept, but it can be rewarding to **embrace the motion of the sky by painting en plein air**.

I have tried many times to paint from photo references and almost always I end up going in a different direction. I will paint it differently because the photo does not give me the essence of a sky - scale and dynamic movement. These elements have to be experienced first-hand. This means getting an impression of what is going on and sticking to that idea while rapidly painting the sky.

Wind, clouds and constantly changing light can become an exciting challenge when you are outdoors with a blank canvas to fill. I find that my painting speeds up. I am laying on the paint in thick dabs or long brushstrokes while looking rapidly from subject to palette and canvas. **The result is usually more interesting that a long session in the studio overworking a photo reference.**

Painting the sky today is a challenge because everything is changing rapidly due to strong winds. The light keeps coming out one moment then being obscured by clouds. All I can do is paint instinctively and that iss a lot of fun!
(Notes in my diary)

A few pointers -

- Mornings and late afternoons are best as the light gives shape to clouds and the colours are richer.

- Watch edges of clouds and try to keep them diffuse.

- Try to keep the sun behind you if you want to see blue sky instead of washed out sky.

- Observe shadows in the clouds depending on the direction of the light so that the clouds have shape.

- Most importantly be guided by what is out there instead of painting symbols of clouds. No fluffy sheep floating about!

- Try to get the sense of movement and light rather than perfectly accurate clouds.

  Have fun!

Chapter 35

Resolutions

New Year.

A time to consider a few resolutions? I cannot recall ever writing down specific resolutions. This is surely the wrong way to go about making resolutions

I need to make a change. I resolve to write down my resolutions this year. This is very doable so I am off to a good start. Next up is getting the resolve to follow through. This is the problem area. You can go wrong here for several reasons.

Distractions make focusing on your goals difficult. Consider that we live in the age of distractions, which makes it difficult to follow through on a goal. Get rid of distractions: TV, smartphone addiction, and any other activity that is not taking you in the right direction. It is a distraction.

Then there is waiting until conditions are just right. For example getting a solid body of work together for an exhibition. (Heck, even getting a solid body would be a great resolution)

Either the works are not quite ready or I want to get another subject done, but there are other things coming up that need attention. Before long I am putting off the goal until next year. The fact is conditions are never perfect. There is always something else that could be done. The idea is to do it in spite of conditions not being ideal. Then you have action.

What about if you have the desire, but fear a lack of skill holds you back? Or maybe you want a better studio or materials or need some other conditions to be met before getting started? There is only one thing to do. Start with what you have.

Even cavemen who painted with the most basic of materials produced lasting works of beauty. How can we complain with our abundance of art materials? Get started with what you have and it becomes easier.

Do what you can. This is not glamour. It is honest. Take what you have with your passion for creativity and get to work. This sort of attitude will carry you much further and for longer than some grandiose resolution that never sees the light of day.

Yes it is good to have a few ideas of what you want for the year. Perhaps you are visualising them as you read this? But most of all, be resolved to start now with what you have. The rest will follow at the right time and place. That, I think, is how the universe works and gives you a chance for success.

Happy New Year!

Chapter 36

Do Artists Live in Fantasy Land?

While browsing through Pinterest recently, I came across a quote that suggested that artists lived in their fantasy land and should be pleased about it.

On the face of it, this seemed like standard dogma. Heck anyone trying to make a living from painting pictures must be living in fantasy land right? Not so fast.

Some may be cruel about it and call artists delusional. I am not sure if anyone would have called Picasso delusional without coming off second best. Many artists come to mind who, I imagine, would put up a vigorous argument that they have a firm grip on reality.

In truth, an artist must strike a balance between creativity, imagination and reality. To succeed, the artist must have focus. A steely determination is called for even in the face of criticism from loved ones. A large ego? Perhaps, but that is not what I mean here. A grip on reality does not require ego. It requires **humility, acceptance and resolve instead.**

Julia Cameron, author of the acclaimed *The Artist's Way*, writes that an artist's creativity is grounded in reality. The artist cannot be distracted by pretense and arrogance. Nor timidity.

Instead, the artist must get an education in the realities of life including such things as marketing, finances and strategy. The artist is a brand and business too. It is foolish to leave these in the hands of third parties.

Every successful artist today has a grip on these realities and must still retain creative innocence. A demanding life indeed.

Now can anyone still suggest that artists are lost in fantasy?

Chapter 37

Free Your Art Spirit

It is a mad man who wears a blindfold then complains that he cannot see. (Pico Iyer)

Is the world getting more conscious of the need for creativity? Experts agree that the world is more than ever divided between rich and poor. What about the divide between artists and the creatively blocked? I say creatively blocked because everyone has a creative side that needs expression in some way.

If more of us acknowledged this creative side and gave it expression then would we not be more balanced people? More fulfilled even?

I have been researching creative issues as part of a new art course that I am working on. One of the surprising results of this research is just how many people want to get in touch with their creative side. What is stopping them?

First off, too many people laugh off art as a joke when put alongside the world's dire issues. I get this because it is a grim situation if one focusses on the TV news.

However, consider how art can uplift communities - both emotionally and economically. What would the impact be on community issues such as crime, unemployment, family breakdown and other psychological issues?

I am suggesting that art and creativity in the wider sense is easier to follow than waiting for expensive government building projects and so on. In short, art is not a trivial subject but can be part of a wider upliftment of society.

What about people who have a secure life, but still struggle to get their art going? **The excuses are common ones.** No time, no money and no talent rank highly. These excuses are tough to challenge because of the emotional firepower that people have to support the excuses. In short, these are symptoms of serious creative blocks that must be faced head-on.

The hardest argument to attack is the one involving money. Yes art is the victim of this issue, but I can assure you that there a plenty of struggling lawyers and other professionals too.

If you believe an idea then it is true for you. That is the way it is. Finally there is no rule that says you have to give up your day job to be an artist. You have the freedom to decide how to run your life. Art does not demand that you sacrifice your financial wellbeing. Art simply requires you to create in order to free your innate spirit. One step at a time.

When to start your creative revival or how is up to you **as long as you begin**. An hour on the weekend? Anyone can manage this.

I can assure you from personal experience that once you begin and commit to the process you will have momentum. This can carry you onward until you build up a regular practice. A creative rebirth opens doors by its very nature. Trust in yourself and the process. Yes, progress may be glacial at first, but we all know the power and impact that is behind such movement.

Art is worth your while. If you find yourself stuck and in doubt remember that it is often one small step that is required to free your art spirit. What if you take that step now?

Chapter 38

This Artist Will Inspire You

He was one of the UK's most successful artists. His beautiful paintings remind one of Pierre Bonnard with their striking colorist influences. He also had one of the coolest names in the art world. Sargy Mann. He was also blind.

Sargy Mann had been an artist his entire adult life. His blindness became permanent in 2005 when he was already an old man. I say old in an objective sense. When you watch the video made by his son Peter Mann you will be amazed by his energy and capacity for work. Find the video on Vimeo.

Even if he still retained his eyesight his accomplishments would have been remarkable. But as a blind man? Well it is nothing short of inspirational.

What really struck me though is when Sargy Mann tells us what happened when he approached his canvas for the first time after complete blindness set in. He explained that he could see the colors clearly. He knew what the painting was in front of him. The colors were vibrant. The shapes manifested in his mind's eye. He was painting and he was enthralled by it. Onlookers were amazed by the painting's beauty too.

This made me realise that when we talk about seeing like an artist we must see intuitively. We must not worry about the details. Like in a dream, we know what we see even though we cannot describe every little detail of what we see. Yet we are in no doubt about what is before us or what we are experiencing. **We lose so much when we rely only on our eyesight.**

Of course Sargy Mann is also an inspiration for his tremendous spirit. His capacity for positive action despite his loss was remarkable. I shall keep it in mind the next time I am in a petulant mood. Get on with it and stop moaning. Remember Sargy Mann!

So take a moment to remember this artist. Sadly he has passed away now, but he lived his art until the end. We can take comfort knowing that we all are capable of much more. We all are so blessed with the talents that we already possess.

Chapter 39

Today You Will Discover More Time to Paint

A regular plea from artists is for more time to paint. Even worse though is the large number of frustrated artists who cannot find the time to even begin painting. Many write to me and say that they wished there was more time to paint. The line is usually: "I would love paint but I just don't have the time." Sometimes I get a reason thrown in like ... because I get home from work and I am too busy/tired etc."

I get this because **I have used these excuses many times**. To be fair, I have on occasion really been under the whip and painting time was impossible. Most times though I was full of it! Yes, procrastination is part of our lives. Distraction is included and GOOD GRIEF are we distracted or what?

This issue became such a problem for me that I took a few drastic measures. **First I took my cell phone off contract** and now I am back to good old pay-as-you-go with airtime only. No data! This means no beep for every email received. No time wasted checking on spam.

Next, after much family debate, we cancelled our TV cable service. Gasp! No more hour or two wasted watching movie reruns every day. The added plus is that, with these two moves, we all get less distracted, have more time for productive stuff and we save a bundle each month! How awesome is that?

The thing is that these moves are very easy to get used to. It is funny recalling how shocked or amused many people were when we cut our television cable service. This was a big deal and they thought we would resume normal service once we had seen the error of our ways. Not even close.

The next issue is telling yourself self-defeating things like "I am so tired!" No we are seldom that tired after work. If there is a fun event waiting for you after work I know that you will find the energy to go do it. Is that not true?

The energy is always there unless we turn it off. This is when we have to decide on **what we want from life**. There is no other option. Time is finite for us mere mortals and it is running out.

There are troves of books devoted to time management. Has anyone ever found the time to finish one? Doubtful. If you find yourself wishing you could start painting, or any other worthwhile activity, please give yourself a break. Start and do not put it off. Do not blame others for stopping you. This is your call.

Oh, and **watch out for the other nasty trap**. This involves rushing to the art store and spending a few grand on materials then never using them. Or enrolling for an art course and not starting or giving up. These moves will hurt your self-esteem. Recognise them and punch them out!

I know it can be tough breaking bad habits, but you can do it. It will be worth it.

Chapter 40

Is Art Just a Product?

When you buy something from an artist, you are buying more than an object. You are buying hundreds of hours of error and experimentation. You are buying years of frustration and moments of pure joy. You are not just buying one thing. You are buying a piece of a heart. A piece of a soul. A small piece of someone else's life.

When I read the words above I thought they were a little dramatic, but had the ring of truth. There is the famous story of a lady who asked Picasso for a portrait. He quickly drew a line on a piece of paper and gave it to her. She was shocked when he asked for a $1,000.00 for the work.

"But it is just a line created in a moment!" she protested.
"Yes, but it comes with a lifetime of experience." replied Picasso.

Artists have to market their work. This is a fact and there can be no complaints about this. We cannot rely on galleries alone. I can communicate to you though this book and I value the independence that this gives me. I think artists enjoy this perk of modern life.

However there are many marketing "teachers" out there who keep on about how our **art is a product**; that artists must get over themselves and accept this reality. Somehow we must now regard our art as stuff to be sold like other goods.

Forgive me for saying this but that is **total rubbish**. If all goods are products to be marketed and sold then where is the art? Surely for something to be art it cannot be just a product churned out on the production line.

Perhaps the original item was art, but if it is copied and replicated over and over then these copies lose their appeal as art.

The above quote said it all for me. There is more to be valued in art than its efficacy as a product. Its ability to match the sofa or fill up that bit of dead space in the passage. A true collector will be moved by art for all those intangible qualities that come with the piece.

So too must the artist value his or her work as more than a product. The value of a painting is more than the paint and canvas. It is more than the price too, although the price must be fair to artist and collector.

In the end I am grateful that **art is the very thing that makes us uniquely human**. That has true value. It would be a pity to forget this.

Chapter 41

Use Paint as the French Use Butter

Generously! Kevin Macpherson said it best when he wrote that we should use paint by the pound and miles of canvas. I love that idea.

If my paintings may lack in composition or some other quality, at least they should not be called stingy in paint. Like the French who insist that good cooking demands rich ingredients, we artists need to be bold with paint and brushstrokes.

The brushstroke is an essential part of this idea. Hold the brush horizontal to the canvas, for example, and lay the paint down in a sideways motion. There should be a textured color note with each stroke. Resist going back over that stroke to avoid flattening it. Use this approach with some variation where necessary, but try not to lose the effect. A distinct mark of color.

Many a time I have finished a painting dissatisfied with the result. Then to return the following day with a fresh eye and was able to appreciate the music of color notes and texture of the oil paint. It is something that seldom disappoints.

Nature, after all, is never flat. Why should our paintings be flat? This week focus your eye on paint and how to apply it. Think of the colour notes that you put down. Do they add to the music or do they detract from the overall harmony?

If your paint is usually thin, then try laying it down thicker. Use a larger brush and seek out the shapes of colour. Does this approach stretch your imagination? Does it delight you or appall you? Good – at least it does not bore you. Keep on.

Chapter 42

The Artist's Path to Mastery

Have you ever wondered what a master artist thinks when the final touch to a work of sublime wonder is complete? What, for example, did Michelangelo think when his sculpture of David was completed? Were his thoughts along the lines of: "Gosh that is great?" Did he see a flaw and feel that he could have done better?

While us mere mortals can only believe that the hand of God guided Michelangelo's chisel, in the end the sculpture is still lifeless marble. Michelangelo probably would have felt that he still had more to say in his artist's journey. That is the way it has to be.

What are the stages to mastery? According to a theory made famous in Malcolm Gladwell's Book, *Outliers*, **mastery takes about ten thousand hours of work**. This amounts to years of dedication to the task.

> *"Practice isn't the thing you do once you're good. It's the thing you do that makes you good."*
> — *Malcolm Gladwell, Outliers: The Story of Success*

Does the thought of ten thousand hours scare you or inspire you? That is the question and if you are honest with yourself the answer can be liberating.

If you paint for a hobby or pastime then you need not worry about mastery. Let things happen as they will and enjoy the present moment.

When you are asked, "What do you do?" Do you reply, "I am an artist"? Then you may be following the road to mastery. It is your life's purpose.

The nice thing to remember is that achieving mastery for this person is not a miserable task. It is what you choose to do because you love it. You design a new computer system in your garage and one day your computers cover the world (think Bill Gates).

Perhaps one day you look around you and see the walls of your house covered with paintings and note that hundreds have been sold to people all over the world. It simply happens over time and it may seem effortless in hindsight.

"Hard work is a prison sentence only if it does not have meaning. Once it does, it becomes the kind of thing that makes you grab your wife around the waist and dance a jig."
— *Malcolm Gladwell, Outliers: The Story of Success*

What are the stages to mastery? These stages have been described as:

Unconscious incompetence
Conscious Incompetence
Conscious Competence
Unconscious Competence

I was looking at a painting by Winslow Homer called *Veteran in a New Field*. You may recall it; it shows a farmer standing cutting wheat with his scythe. It is so simple in composition yet it compels me to look at it in fascination.

The painting can mean many things: A simple scene of farmer cutting wheat? A testimony to the end of war and a return to peace and plenty? A sense of unease with one man facing a sea of work, but remaining poor in the process? A harbinger of trouble ahead? A metaphor for the fallen?

Whatever the meaning is to you, it is the work of a master artist. That is why **following the path to mastery is so important for everyone**. The stages of competence cannot be avoided. Accept them and know that your persistence will be joyful and enriching. If you can face each day with anticipation and energy to get stuck in then you have found your purpose.

When you have your purpose figured out then your journey is simpler. The mastery is not a destination like the next train station. It is the journey that matters.

You are an inspiration to others and your work benefits others too. That is the way life is meant to be. Simple when you think about it isn't it?

> *"My earliest memories of my father are of seeing him work at his desk and realizing that he was happy. I did not know it then, but that was one of the most precious gifts a father can give his child."*
> — *Malcolm Gladwell, Outliers: The Story of Success*

Chapter 43

Art is not a Balancing Act

Has someone told you that you need to live a balanced life? Eat balanced meals and balance your finances? It seems balance is a big deal since we all are told to bring balance into our life. Yet what picture does this conjure up in your mind?

I know that balance suggests 50/50. The scales of commerce seek to balance out to equal sums. Fail to balance your account and there is a problem. But this image is all wrong about life. To hit the sweet spot in life, as in art, we need to be forget about equal scales.

The fifty/fifty idea of balance is boring and potentially confusing. It is beige in colour and associated with sitting on the fence. It is in fact a dangerous notion. Think of financial well-being. It is better to have more assets than liabilities. If you are out of balance in this way you are financially secure. If you are in the fifty/fifty zone then a slight financial commitment can send you toppling over in debt.

In art there is the Golden Section. That natural ideal found in all things. This roughly translates to one third to two thirds as an ideal composition in painting or photography. Consider most paintings and photographs that employ the golden section.

. The asymmetrical composition is pleasing and calming. Place the focal point in the middle and there is often a pictorial tension.

If our daily lives are to have meaning and fulfillment then **we need to reject balance and rather focus on one thing above all others**. What is the one thing that is your passion? What is the one thing that will pull your life into the path of success? That is the area to focus energy and committed action. If it is art then devour as much as you can. Paint a lot. Study and paint more. That is the way to make real progress.

Too much can also be harmful. Yes the Golden Section allows a generous one-third for other activities so there is a counter weight to your passion work. So long as you have the most effort going to that one critical area of your life.

We have to be aware of where our energy is focused. If you are not making real progress and you feel that you are drifting then you are probably not committed to that one thing. Figure this out and renew your energy for that single pursuit and you will see real results.

Chapter 44

The Wonderful World of an Artist's Journal

Ever wanted to do something artistic, but did not know where to start? Are you in a creative rut? Did you draw a lot as a child, but have you now drifted away from this pleasure? Maybe it is time to try journaling!

Oh yes, I know it may sound frivolous to talk about keeping a journal. You know it sounds like a talk-show affirmation: I will keep a journal next to my bed and ... But take a look on Pinterest at the examples of artist's journals. You will see how big this trend has become. The quality of work in some cases is jaw-dropping, but do not let that intimidate you. Art journals are for anyone even slightly interested in drawing.

Artist's journals are part drawing, painting, illustration and writing. They can be free form or follow a specific theme. Keep them in notebooks, loose leaf pages or napkins. You can write in them daily, on specific events like holiday travels or for a weekly recap on your life. Whatever works for you is fine.

How to get started? Keeping it simple is always best. A few water resistant pens. A notebook with unlined paper. Perhaps some watercolor pencils or a small pan of watercolor pigments if color is important to you. Then start drawing. Add some notes on what inspired your drawing. Let the mood take you.

My sketching kit is simple indeed. A pencil roll-up containing water resistant pens (05 and 08 Pigma micron) a selection of Staedtler watercolor pencils, a watercolor brush and an A5 Eco journal.

If I want to, I may use a watercolor palette, but that is mostly for studio work. I may add to this kit, but I enjoy the no frills nature of it compared to the baggage that goes with an oil painting kit.

Some artists record their travel adventures. Others their daily work. It can become a cathartic process of unburdening what is holding you down. Free-form writing can do that to you.

I like the simplicity of the process. **It is something that connects me to my childhood days**. I sketched compulsively as a child. Copied panels from comics. Made up my own comics too. Now I can draw for possible painting references. I draw while sitting at the kitchen table chatting to my wife.

Drawing what exactly?

Whatever catches my eye is a worthy subject. A bottle of beer, a box of matches, the family dog sitting nearby - whatever grabs my attention. Another plus is that it makes outdoor work very easy for the introverts (like me). Sketch at the coffee shop, park, beach or bench at the mall. It is plein air without the stress.

If the bug bites then **look for inspiration from other sketchers**. Look at urbansketchres.org and marvel at the beautiful journals. When you feel ready start your own blog and post pictures now and then of your work. Who knows where it may lead?

There are many sketchers online to inspire you too. For example Tommy Kane has a fun blog full of stories and drawings. While visiting the urban sketchers blog, I came across a correspondent for Africa. In fact, the only correspondent for Africa is a South African namely Cathy Gatland. I am sure we can increase that number! Anyone volunteering? You can follow this link if you are keen to join.

I hope that inspired you to give sketching a go. Please send me a note of your progress if you like.
Have fun!

Chapter 45

How to Grow Your Creative Career

*Perseverance is not a long race. It
is many short races one after the
other. (Walter Elliot)*

**Conventional business suggests that the bigger the
statement the better the result.** Other ideas like *Go Big or
Go Home* add to this belief. When there is plenty at stake it
is easy to believe this concept. After all, we want our
business to succeed. We bundle up our self-worth into
succeeding at our venture.

Examples of how this idea has caused me harm are:

1. Jumping into a bad business partnership despite clear
    warnings not to. Clear only if I was taking the trouble
    to look.
2. Renting fancy business premises when cash-flow was
    tight.
3. Employing bad people when I should be doing the
    work myself. Dear God, never again!
4. Not saving or investing sooner because there were
    more exciting things to do. Buy. Experience.
    Rationalise this any way you like. It will catch up to
    you and bite.
5. Spending too much on marketing that did not convert.
    This thanks to misplaced ego or laziness.

The list can go on. Perhaps you recognise a few of them or they jog your memory of painful times.

None of these proved fatal although they cost me time and money. I was able to take my medicine and kept trying. The big lesson was evident. **It is what you do over time that matters**.

It is the ripples you make over time that break through the barriers. The big waves? They are over quickly and cause destruction. The ripples get the appreciation and the results.

In nature, we see the canyons, tall trees and abundant wildlife created over time. Sound boring? Exciting results come from persistence, commitment and doing your homework. On their own these qualities are not glamorous. They are however, what makes entrepreneurs succeed.

In the art world, glamour gets most of the attention but persistence wins. The artist who gets to work every day is going to succeed over time. This is the rule of nature and the universe.

Of course **artists are entrepreneurs**. Acting on an idea, creating something where there was nothing, taking calculated risks. Putting yourself out there. These are all qualities of the entrepreneur. It pays to have vision and the patience to make it happen over time.

Some may ask: "Why go slowly in this fast paced world? **Should we not be hustling like crazy to survive?"** I will take social media as an example. I am not an expert on the topic, but when I read the views of experts they seem to say the same thing. Use what works for you and persist at it.

Is your market on Pinterest or Facebook? Then focus on that media and persist with sharing your good work. Over the long haul. You will be standing when the others have given up.

Only your good work though. Leave out the stuff that pulls you down. Remember consistency? We trust consistency. We want to trust you.

My message here is a personal one from many attempts and failures over time. Those things that worked turned out to be common sense after all. The key was to keep trying new ideas. Keep learning and be honest with myself. What is delusion and ego? What is real and true? Learn the difference and keep putting it out there little by little.

Chapter 46

20 Ways to Find More Creativity and Inspiration

Creative block takes many forms. Boredom or simply frustration and lack of motivation all point to one thing - A block to your creative process. If you can work through this, it often means a step-up to new and successful ventures. Here are a few ways to make this breakthrough happen faster:

1. **Prepare for inspiration** by doing the mundane. Tasks like priming the canvases, sweeping the studio or cleaning brushes lead to action. The bonus is that you will be ready for it!
2. **Turn off the TV.** It will waste your time and dull your senses. Any other gadget that wastes your time? Same thing.
3. **Declutter.** Even for ten minutes. Clear a desk. Throw away empty paint tubes. Unused boxes and stuff you are keeping in case you need it. Clutter blocks energy. This has a real influence on your creativity.
4. **Let others inspire you.** Do you have any uber-creative friends or mentors? If not find someone in books or online that inspires you. Yes, seek inspiration from others who have it in spades and feel that energy. Put it into action.
5. **Bribe yourself.** Promise yourself a treat if you complete a project. A new book to read if you finish the painting. Watch the DVD once you complete writing that chapter and so on.

6. **Use lists.** Some people like lists. If this works for you then put your task on the list. "Start painting today" then put in the mundane items. Always include your creative task with the other to do items. Keep the list short. Three main items a day. Anything else is a bonus but OK to leave off.
7. **Make someone's day.** Giving is better than receiving. It fills you with energy and this leads to creativity. Give a small gift of your art. Help someone. Pay it forward. Whatever gives you a feel-good charge of energy?
8. **Exercise.** Walks, biking, dancing or whatever makes you move. Best done outdoors. I enjoy a walk on the beach and climbing the tallest dune. The view is amazing and the exercise gets the creative mood going.
9. **Music.** Listening to music may work for you. Music does influence emotions so try something that makes you happy.
10. **Simplify.** Clear your day if there are too many demands to meet. Simplify your life? Toxic situations in your life? Move on. Life is too short.
11. **Try something new.** Maybe you are stuck with a certain technique because it sells? Try something different for fun and see where it leads.
12. **Travel.** Whether far or near. New sights and experiences stimulate the creative energy. Be open to experience these new things.
13. **Talk** to other artists. Everyone can share their ideas and experiences. You are not alone.
14. **Play Hooky!** Maybe you need to take some time off. This treat can give you the spark you need. Plus a little guilt will get you working harder.
15. **Meditate.** The noise of everyday life can get too much. Step away and breathe using basic meditation techniques. Find a peaceful place with no interruptions.
16. **Free Doodle.** Using any materials without any plan. Just draw or paint big shapes. Loose and free. Be open to ideas as they come forward on their own.

17. **Visualise.** See what you want and you will set the process in motion. This is a powerful method and will help you take the next step whatever it may be.
18. **Journal.** Write your daily thoughts. Illustrate them. Simply putting your thoughts on paper is a way of clearing mental clutter.
19. **Start a Mood Board.** Preferably the analog version. Pinterest is okay, but it is too easy on its own. A physical board will engage you more deeply.
20. **Start!** Taking action, whatever that may mean for you, creates its own momentum. Once you get moving the inspiration will start flowing again.

Inspired? Take this week to test out one of these suggestions.

Chapter 47

How Painting Saved Winston Churchill

Happy are the painters for they never shall be lonely. Light and colour; peace and hope shall keep them company to the end – or almost the end of the day.

(Winston Churchill)

What image does the name Winston Churchill conjure up in your mind? For many it will be the iconic pictures of Churchill, cigar clamped in his jaw, looking determined as he faces down the war time threat to Britain's freedom. Perhaps the victory sign raised to cheering crowds after VE Day?

Churchill is the symbol of British tenacity in the face of great threat. But there were many sides to Churchill's character including great sensitivity.

I recently had the pleasure of reading Winston Churchill's book *Painting as a Pastime*. It is a short book, but reveals a side of Churchill that few have appreciated. That a figure of such magnitude would write about painting says much about his character and the virtues of art.

In 1915 Churchill faced an uncertain political future. He was at his lowest ebb after a few unsuccessful years in the military. He found himself sidelined and depressed. It was at this juncture, in his early forties, that he decided to try painting for the first time. Churchill took to painting with, in his own words, great audacity.

With the help of an artist friend, Churchill learned how **to defeat the tyranny of a white canvas**. Churchill would administer "several large, fierce strokes" with a large brush on the cowering canvas. He never felt in awe of a canvas since then. No fiddling with little brushes with a meek heart. Get stuck in and enjoy the release that painting brings to mind and soul

Churchill had **a strong attraction to oil painting** over watercolor. The versatility and power of oils appealed to his nature. Plus Churchill appreciated that mistakes could be adjusted or even scraped away with ease. A point I can endorse!

Churchill sought to achieve a **balance between work and play** long before this idea became trendy. Painting was the ideal distraction from the demands of politics.

The right-brain remedy of painting was essential to his effectiveness as a leader. There is no doubt that Churchill needed painting to save him from a difficult time in his life. Plus painting restored his energies when he faced the extraordinary demands of wartime leadership.

Painting helped Churchill enjoy nature more.

"I think this heightened sense of observation of Nature is one of the chief delights that have come to me through trying to paint." Painting outdoors delighted Churchill: "Go out into the sunlight and be happy with what you see."

Was there any better way to keep occupied than painting?

"Armed with a paint-box, one cannot be bored, one cannot be left at a loose end, one cannot have several days on one's hands."

It is interesting to note **Churchill's fascination with impressionism and post-impressionists**. Remember that these movements were still new in the 1920's. Churchill loved strong color and bold shapes. He said that artists like Manet, Monet, Cezanne and Matisse "have brought back to the pictorial art a new draught of *joie de vivre*."

Painting was not only about enjoyment for Churchill. He appreciated **the health benefits** to body and mind too. "What a useful exercise painting may be for the development of an accurate and retentive memory."

What better way to **distract a troubled mind** than painting. "I know of nothing which, without exhausting the body, more entirely absorbs the mind. Whatever the worries of the hour or threats of the future, once the picture has begun to flow there is no room for them in the mental screen"

Winston Churchill became **an accomplished painter,** producing over 500 paintings. He also exhibited at the British Royal Academy. If Churchill could find the time to paint then we all can.

This short book reminded me that even in these cynical times, painting is a wonderful **cure for the mind and spirit** for all ages.

For example, children can express their creativity away from gadgets. What about stressed executives, those facing boredom, middle-age angst or old age worries? Painting will help. But don't take my word for it. Take it from Winston Churchill and get yourself a paint-box today.

Chapter 48

Being an Artist Makes You Question Everything

What separates the talented individual from the successful one is a lot of hard work. (Stephen King)

When you decide to call yourself an artist, things begin to change. A shift begins from the idea of being an artist to actually living the life of an artist. You start to question what you do and what you think you should do. If you are not careful you will find yourself questioning everything. This can unsettle you, but it is also necessary.

Here are a few examples:

There are the mental questions:

1)   **Are you good enough?** Does your work justify calling yourself an artist or are you a pretender? This one causes damage, but you will have to confront it and banish it. Expect it to crop up again.

2)   **What is good enough anyway?** Who gets to decide? Is it you, your friends, strangers? You will confront issues like the depth of your talent.

Is it all innate or can you get better? How to measure talent? Is it through critical acclaim or prizes or art sales?

3) **Is your education sound?** Do you need a degree or can you be self-taught? Sometimes the absence of formal education can undermine an artist's self-esteem. You will need to put this aside to overcome self-doubt. The answer? What you learn through experience is the most important.

4) **Do you make art your career** or moonlight on the side? Do you transition from formal job to full time artist? These strategic decisions are critical. It starts with deciding what you want from your life. The answer should follow, but it could take years to unravel.

5) **What is your vision?** Your lifestyle, your work and your rewards all stem from your vision. Take time to work this out and write it down. Make it your own.

There are Practical questions:

1) **What genre should you focus on?** This can have financial implications for artists going professional. At the same time you have to be honest with your creative spirit. The idea of compromise is unattractive to artists, but often it is a means to an end.

2) **What medium to use?** Materials to source and quality impacts the bottom line. What are you comfortable with and where do you need to challenge your comfort zone.

3)   **Finances.** What is your budget for materials and running a studio? Can you put a price on wastage and figure out what is costing you money? If you cannot measure it, you cannot fix it.

4)   **Time management.** Do you spend enough time doing what is important? Nothing is more important than time actually creating. Without this there will not be mastery of your art. Your art will improve with committed and focused work.

5)   **Marketing.** Learn this through trial and error. Where and who is your market? If you do not have a real plan then you will waste more time and money than necessary.

6)   **How much** to spend on marketing? Less than you may think, but test returns on time and money.

7)   **Galleries or self-marketing?** Most artists will have to make their own waves. Best to learn this this from the get go and keep your freedom. But do not burn bridges either.

8)   **Do you know yourself?** For example how much do you need to live on? This comes down to knowing what you need. Plus what is going out your wallet and what comes in.

9)   **Income.** Can some of it be passive income? What intellectual property can work for you when you are sleeping? Multiple streams of income is the new model to consider.

10) **Teaching?** Pass on your knowledge generously and it will pay you back in the long run.

11) **Do you need help?** Seek a mentor. Take courses and read books. Never stop learning, because you do not know it all.

12) **Remain relevant** by making yourself relevant. Harsh but true. You decide. That is the good part.

There are many other questions. If you are asking questions then you are also finding answers. This makes life fulfilling and you are not a passenger. In the end I know that I will never know everything. I hope I leave this world still curious and hungry for more to discover.

Chapter 49

Is Passion the Key to Success?

It can be hard to accept, but being a passionate artist is not enough if you want to make a living from it. This applies to anything I guess, but let me stay with art for now

. There are many quotes, books and articles about following your passion. Everybody hates their day job. It is such a drag. Would it not be better to follow your passion? You know what I mean? So quit your job and follow your passion. This is misleading advice!

Let me be honest and admit that I have accepted this challenge for a long time. I do want to make a living doing what I am passionate about. My friends and family would love me to be happy doing what I am passionate about. That is fine. Plenty of moral support. But let me not forget. Making art is not enough.

The reality check is that art must be good and it must be in demand. The economics must be there. Supply and demand applies to art too. Awful I know, but exciting when it works out.

So what does an artist do? It has nothing to do with fine art degrees for a start. I will hone this down to painters for the sake of argument. Art has many directions and some are more commercial than others. Designers of products may find commercial success easier than portrait artists for example.

So our painter paints paintings. With passion. He or she loves painting and wants to paint every day. Everybody would agree that this artist has a passion for painting. Yet nobody purchases the paintings. Pretty soon our artist must make some tough decisions. Carry on painting? Get a day job? Give up painting except for a hobby? Study for a conventional career?

Now I am a sucker for a good ending. I love rags-to-riches stories. I am fascinated by artists who have done well for themselves. But I get it. Passion is not enough. I have experienced this first hand. The cold hard truth is that, no matter what I try, I had better be good at it if I want to make a living from it. This means the business side too. I must also have people willing to buy my work.

This does not only mean painting well. This is a given. I know you may point at some artists and question why their work is highly paid. This is beside the point.

The point is simple. **One needs to be good at every part of the equation.** Good art. Good business skills. Persistent attention to detail. Never give up. If you can keep on this path then you have passion. But you also have the attitude to see through the long haul. One day your "good" will become great.

At first I did not take this advice with good humour. I did want passion to be enough. Now after years of working in this field I can say that my passion for art has not dimmed. I have grown up though. I will not be too proud to earn from other sources if required. We all have to do what is necessary at the time and move on.

The conclusion is this: Passion is not enough. You need to bring the whole package if you want to make a living from what you enjoy. With this knowledge you can go ahead and make it happen.

Chapter 50

Artist Paint is Expensive so Use More of It

I am sure that you love to paint. But when you stand in front of the paint display at your art shop what goes through your mind when you reach for those new tubes? I am pretty sure that you are doing some quick multiplication. Maybe you don't need so many tubes after all. Not if you want to pay the bills this month.

With import duties and currency troubles artists continue to see big jumps in paint prices. So is the answer is to eke out paint and use it sparingly? Not at all. One of the biggest reasons for paintings that disappoint us is skinny paint. I touched on this in a previous chapter about using paint like the French use butter.

When your painting has such thin paint application you cannot see a ripple of texture. It is flat, blended and weak. Like bad instant coffee. No thanks. I truly believe that when we use skinny paint we get insipid results and we also feel like we are cheating ourselves. When you hold back on the paint are you really expressing your feelings?

Many new artists are also seduced by the large canvas. It is so tempting when we see that large canvas at the shop. One metre wide – Wow! It will look great. Maybe it will, but that is a lot of painting real estate to cover and it takes up a lot of paint. So we paint skinny and feel disappointed with the result.

I would like to suggest that you put away the big canvas and focus on painting with emotion and with a generous spirit. Paint with bravura as the critics say. Lay the paint on thick where the painting calls for it.

Use layers in the light passages. Texture the foreground with that large bristle brush. Use impasto to contrast against thinner passages in the shadows. You get the idea?

This approach will bring you joy and save you paint too. How so?

First off try painting on smaller panels such as 6 x 8" or 10 x 12" at first. Use a relatively large brush like a size 4 and 6 and lay on the paint. Butter it on where necessary. Because you have a small panel to cover you are not using tubes of paint. But your painting will still be rich with thick juicy paint. Gem-like colours glowing and resplendent!

That one small painting will make a bigger statement than a large canvas with skinny paint. Painting this way will also build your confidence. It forces you to make the shapes simpler. More emphasis on big shapes with less detail. This often means stronger value contrasts too. This adds impact. Your compositions will be stronger too. More cropped with only the strong important shapes.

For inspiration look at artists like Kevin Macpherson and Ken

Auster. Artists who work outdoors often will have adopted this approach, because it helps them paint quickly and boldly.

Another tip is to use fewer tube colours. This saves money and reduces the risk of muddy colour mixes. Try working with the primary colours and white. There will be more colour harmony in your mixes plus less wastage. If you have to scrape back then use that scraped off paint for warm or cool grey colour. These greys can set-off your pure colours to great effect.

It is a shame that many artists may feel inhibited by costs. This kind of thinking can spoil the joy of painting. But in truth not painting or holding back is more costly. **When you hold back you pay with your spirit** and that is too high a price. So the challenge is to make the most of your paint. Go small, but go bold!

Chapter 51

The Simple Answer to Productivity

Year-end approaches and everything starts to call for attention. Productivity suffers. Maybe you have holidays in December so you have calculated how many days you have to get things done. The kids will finish school next week so I have to get everything finished before then. So it goes.

Except is doesn't. You find that nothing gets done because you are fretting about what you did not do yesterday. The cat is still at the vet and you have rude messages on the phone from your boss. Apparently it is not okay to arrive 30 minutes late after lunch. Does he even realise how hectic the traffic is this time of year?

You may think that artists have it easy. What with painting, entertaining and contemplation in the off-peak times. Life for us is a doddle. But no. It is fraught with angst too. There are deadlines for commissions. Packing paintings for year-end exhibitions and the usual business paperwork too. Plus the courier company wants their bill paid last week.

Then sales actually start grinding to a halt. Yes, the demands of the festive season can leave most people staring into empty wallets. This creates a severe dent in disposable income to, oh, about May next year. So no joy for artists for a while then. No matter. All this is unimportant in the grand scheme of things. Except for one thing.

The one thing that is important. Put aside all distractions for a moment. Simplify everything so that you can focus on the ONE THING. Which happens to be doing your art. All the running about getting frantic over nonsense does not take your life forward. Your number one focus must be creating your best work. then sharing your work.

Not sure about this? There is a book devoted to this topic. It is well worth the read if you have time that is. There is a similar principle in economics too. The 80/20 rule which says that eighty percent of the returns come from twenty percent of the customers. The trick is knowing who that twenty percent is and what they like. Nothing that a bit of focus cannot solve.

This is also the way to peacefully live your life. Focus on the twenty percent that matters. The rest is distraction. When you get down to the real work your entire being calms down. The act of creating is a real need. You can feed the body, but you cannot ignore the soul.

But what about your business? Remember what made others join your world? It was your art. No matter what you create, think of it as your art. People want this from you. It is also what makes you happy. So do more art.

Give up the rat-race. Ignore the tail-chasing madness. Keep doing the one thing that makes your life complete. Maybe all you need to do today is the one thing.

What do you think?

Chapter 52

Fourteen Reason Why Art Makes an Excellent Christmas Present

It started in October. I walked into the supermarket and at first I did not register that something was amiss. You know that feeling? What is wrong with this picture? What the heck! #$%#^&$ plastic Christmas trees in my way! Tinsel hanging in my face as if installed by tiny elves. Already! It's only October!

I procrastinated throughout October despite my wife's reminders to start looking for gifts. There is no getting away from it now though. It is November. Time to prepare for the festive season.

This means overheating my credit card until it resembles Salvador Dali's pocket watch. Never mind. A few pennies in the red is nothing compared to the beatific smiles of my little urchins on the Christmas morn. Or is it?

As I recall the yuletide past there was not peace and goodwill to all. This was due to a shortage of batteries, the incorrectly sized screwdriver, insufficient RAM and various other technical issues.

So it is time to **rethink gift giving**. A time for radical change. A time for the ideal Christmas gift. A work of art!

Not convinced? Then have a read through this list of 14 reasons why you should give art as a gift:

1. **It is unique**. In a world of cookie-cutter design and packaged clutter, an original painting stands apart.
2. **Love**. Yes! Nothing says I love you like a work of art. Be it romantic or platonic you will be declaring your love for life and all things good. Shameless aren't I?
3. **Support a good cause**. Nobody likes to see starving artists. It makes the place look untidy. Do a good turn and help one out this year. Go on Guv.
4. **Show your true colours**. Tired of people looking at you like you have no culture. Is binge-watching TV your raison d'être? Then purchasing fine art will shut up the plebs once and for all.
5. **It takes time**. This is a double-edged sword. Time is precious. Yet taking some time to discern fine art is good for the soul. So we're good then.
6. **No Batteries required**. This may be the only reason you ever need!
7. **No upgrades required**. Giving the latest computer game? Think again. You or the recipient will have to spend a fortune upgrading the computer.
8. **No assembly required.** Few things annoy a semi-sober spouse more than trying to assemble a gift. It will lead to tears or at least swearing at the kids.
9. **Watching the recipient's reaction**. This may be a fun moment depending on how it turns out. Tip: do a little research on the recipient's taste of art.
10. **It lasts into the New Year**. Longer if it is not a paper mache installation. Yes, a work of art can last generations while all other gifts have hit the bin. How many gifts even make it into the New Year?
11. **No noise**. A painting gets on with it without any noise. Not so Michael Buble's newish Christmas album. Nuff said!

12. **Non-fattening**. Often you find that you have outgrown your clothing by New Year. Thanks to boxes of chocs, biscuits and fortified drinks the waistline suffers a bit. Instead, give a fat-free painting. Hanging a painting qualifies as exercise too. Dr Oz would be proud!
13. **Cost Effective too**. Avoid the naysayers. They may suggest that art can be pricey. Unfriend the Philistines!
14. **Because you are worth it**. What about you? You have toiled and sacrificed all year. Do they appreciate it? Course not. Now it is time to spoil yourself. A beautiful work of art is a just reward.

So there it is. My shameless and unrepentant list of why art makes the perfect Christmas gift. If you will spare my blushes I can suggest that you visit my website and splurge.

Happy Christmas everyone and a fab New Year!

About the Author

Malcolm Dewey is an artist and author living in South Africa with his wife, Kerrin Dewey, also an author. They have three sons.

Malcolm paints in a contemporary impressionist style. His subjects are mostly landscapes and figure studies. He paints regularly and has collectors from all over the world.

A part of this creative drive is to teach painting to as many others as he can. The world needs more artists too! To accomplish this Malcolm has several painting courses available online, has an active YouTube channel (mdfineart) and writes about art.

Please connect with Malcolm:
Website: Http://www.malcolmdeweyfineart.com
YouTube/mdfineart
Facebook/MalcolmDeweyFineArt

Plus his popular podcast:
An Artist's Journey Podcast

Enjoy a free painting course when you join Malcolm's Artist's and Collector's Circle on his website.

Acknowledgements

I do want to thank the many artists who have contributed to my creative growth over the years. Many of the stories and advice written about in this book are inspired by questions, feedback and interaction with these artists.

In particular those of you that have joined my Artist's and Collector's Circle I have a special thank you for your support and enthusiasm. Without that relationship an artist's life can get a little isolated.

Special Mention: I am grateful to Susan Wilkinson for her help in editing this book, her keen eye to spot elusive errors and enthusiastic support for this project. Also my gratitude to Alene Blythe for her help in correcting errors that did elude my eye.

Thank you for reading this book. If you enjoyed it please leave your review.

All the best

Malcolm

Printed in Poland
by Amazon Fulfillment
Poland Sp. z o.o., Wrocław

60545605R00092